Babylonian Assyrian Birth Omens

And

Their Cultural Significance

by
Morris Jastrow
Ph. D. (Leipzig) Professor of Semitic Languages in the University of Pennsylvania (Philadelphia)

To

SIR WILLIAM OSLER

Regius Professor of Medicine
Oxford University

This volume is dedicated
as a mark of esteem and admiration.

"Most fine, most honour'd, most renown'd."
(King Henry V, 2d Part, Act IV, 5, 164.)

Analysis

Divination in Babylonia and Assyria

Three chief methods: hepatoscopy, astrology and birth-omens

Spread of Hepatoscopy and Astrology to Hittites, Etruscans, Greeks and Romans and to China

The Transition motif in religious rites and popular customs

Omen collections in Ashurbanapal's Library

Birth-omen reports

Animal Birth-omens

Double foetus

Principles of interpretation

Multiple births among ewes

Malformation of ears

Excess number of ears

Ewe giving birth to young resembling lion

Ewe giving birth to young resembling other animals

Human Birth-omens

Twins

Monstrosities

Multiple births

Malformation of ears

Malformation of mouth, nostrils, jaws, arms, lips, hand

Malformation of anus, genital member, thigh, feet

Principles of interpretation

Misshapen embryos

Weaklings, cripples, deaf-mutes, still-births, dwarfs

Talking infants, with bearded lips and teeth

Infants with animal features

Study of Human Physiognomy among Greeks and Romans

Resemblances between human and animal features

Porta's and Lavater's Views

Study of Human Physiognomy based on birth-omens

Birth-omens in Julius Obsequens

Birth-omens in Valerius Maximus

Cicero on birth-omens

Macrobius on birth-omens

Birth-omens among Greeks and in Asia Minor

Birth-omens as basis of belief in fabulous and hybrid beings

Dragons, Hippocentaurs and hybrid creatures in Babylonian-Assyrian Literature and Art

Fabulous creatures of Greek Mythology and Birth-omens

Egyptian sphinxes

Totemism

Metamorphosis of human beings into animals and vice versa

Talking animals in fairy tales

History of monsters and persistency of belief in monsters

Lycosthenes' work

Summary

Index

"... they do observe
unfather'd heirs and loathly births of natures"

(King Henry V. 2nd part
Act IV, 4, 121-122).

I

As a result of researches in the field of Babylonian-Assyrian divination, now extending over a number of years[1], it may be definitely said that apart from the large class of miscellaneous omens[2], the Babylonians and Assyrians developed chiefly three methods of divination into more or less elaborate systems—divination through the inspection of the liver of a sacrificial animal or Hepatoscopy, through the observation of the movements in the heavens or Astrology, (chiefly directed to the moon and the planets but also to the sun and the prominent stars and constellations), and through the observance of signs noted at birth in infants and the young of animals or Birth-omens. Elsewhere[3], I have suggested a general division of the various forms of divination methods into two classes, voluntary and involuntary divination, meaning by the former the case in which a sign is deliberately selected and then observed, by the latter where

---

[1] Embodied in detail in the author's *Religion Babyloniens und Assyriens* II 203-969 to be referred to hereafter as Jastrow *Religion*. See also various special articles by the writer such as "Signs and Names for the Liver in Babylonian" (Zeitschr. f. Assyr. XX 105-129). "The Liver in Antiquity and the Beginnings of Anatomy" (Trans. of the College of Physicians of Phila. XXIX 117-138). "The Liver in Babylonian Divination" (Proc. of the Numismatic and Antiquarian Soc. of Phila. XXV 23-30). "The Liver as the Seat of the Soul" (Studies in the History of Religions presented to C. H. Toy 143-169). "Sign and Name for Planet in Babylonian" (Proc. Amer. Philos. Society XLVII 141-156). "Hepatoscopy and Astrology in Babylonia and Assyria" (ib. XLVII 646-676). "Sun and Saturn" (Revue d'Assyriologie VII No. 2), and the general survey in the author's *Aspects of Religious Belief and Practice in Babylonia and Assyria* (N. Y. 1911), Chapter III and IV.

[2] The field of divination was gradually extended so that practically every unusual occurrence or every occurrence that even aroused attention was regarded as an omen. Among these miscellaneous classes of omens we may distinguish as distinct subdivisions (a) dreams, (b) phenomena connected with rivers and canals, (c) movements of animals—chiefly serpents, dogs, sheep and certain birds like ravens and falcons; also mice and rats, and various insects as roaches and locusts, (d) phenomena in houses and temples, including probably (as in Leviticus, Chap. 14) suspicious looking marks or spots, (e) peculiarities and diseases of any portion of the human frame. No doubt the list can be still further extended.

[3] See Hepatoscopy and Astrology in Babylonia and Assyria (Proc. Amer. Philos. Society XLVII 646 sq.)

the sign is not of your own choice but forced upon your attention and calling for an interpretation. Hepatoscopy falls within the former category[4], Astrology and Birth-omens in the latter.

Each one of these three methods rests on an underlying well-defined theory and is not the outcome of mere caprice or pure fancy, though of course these two factors are also prominent. In the case of Hepatoscopy, we find the underlying theory to have been the identification of the 'soul' or vital centre of the sacrificial victim—always a sheep—with the deity to whom the animal is offered,—at least to the extent that the two souls are attuned to one another. The liver being, according to the view prevalent among Babylonians and Assyrians as among other peoples of antiquity at a certain stage of culture, the seat of the soul[5], the inspection of the liver followed as the natural and obvious means of ascertaining the mind, i. e., the will and disposition of the deity to whom an inquiry has been put or whom one desired to consult. The signs on the liver—the size and shape of the lobes, and of the gall bladder, the character or peculiarities of the two appendices to the upper lobe, (the processus pyramidalis and the processus papillaris), and the various markings on the liver were noted, and on the basis of the two main principles conditioning all forms of divination (1) association of ideas and (2) noting the events that followed upon certain signs, a decision was reached as to whether the deity was favorably or unfavorably disposed or, what amounted to the same thing, whether the answer to the inquiry was favorable or unfavorable.

In the case of Astrology,—a relatively more advanced method of divination,—the underlying theory rested on the supposed complete correspondence between movements and phenomena in

---

[4] The Greek and Roman method of sending out birds and noting their flight is another example of voluntary divination, and so is the ancient Arabic method of selecting arrows, writing certain words on them, throwing them before the image or symbol of a deity and as they fell, reading the oracle sent by the deity.

[5] See the details in the writer's 'The Liver as the Seat of the Soul'. (Toy Anniversary volume 143-168.)

the heavens and occurrences on earth. The gods, being identified with the heavenly bodies,—with the moon, sun, planets, and fixed stars—or as we might also put it, the heavenly bodies being personified as gods, the movements in the heavens were interpreted as representing the activity of the gods preparing the events on earth. Therefore, he who could read the signs in the heavens aright would know what was to happen here below. Astrology corresponded in a measure to the modern Weather Bureau in that it enabled one to ascertain a little in advance what was certain to happen, sufficiently so in order to be prepared for it. Compared with Hepatoscopy, Astrology not only represents a form of divination that might be designated as semi-scientific—only relatively scientific of course—but also occupies a higher plane, because there was no attempt involved to induce a deity unfavorably disposed to change his mind. The signs were there; they pointed unmistakably to certain occurrences on earth that were certain to occur and it was the task of the diviner—the bârû or 'inspector' as the Babylonian called him—to indicate whether what the gods were preparing would be beneficial or harmful. Both Hepatoscopy and Astrology as developed by the Babylonians and Assyrians bârû-priests exerted a wide influence, the former spreading to the Hittites and Etruscans and through the one or the other medium to Greeks and Romans[6], while Babylonian-Assyrian Astrology passing to the Greeks became the basis for Graeco-Roman and mediaeval Astrology, profoundly influencing the religious thought of Europe[7] and in a modified form surviving even to our own days. The chain of evidence has recently been completed[8] to prove the direct transfer of the cuneiform astrological literature to Greek astrologers and

---

[6] See Jastrow, *Religion* II 120 sq. and "The Liver as the Seat of the Soul" (Toy Anniversary volume) 158-165.
[7] See Cumont, *Fatalisme Astrale et Religions Antiques* (Revue d'Histoire et de Littérature Religieuse 1912); also the same author's *Astrology and Religion among the Greeks and Romans* (N. Y. 1912).
[8] Bezold and Boll, *Reflexe astrologischer Keilschriften bei griechischen Schriftstellern* (Heidelberg Akad. d. Wiss. 1911); see also Cumont, *Babylon und die griechische Astronomie* (Neue Jahrbücher f. das klass. Altertum XXVIII Abt. I. 1-10).

astronomers. The possibility also of a spread or at least of a secondary influence of both systems to the distant East is also to be considered. In fact considerable evidence is now available to show that Babylonian-Assyrian astrological notions and in part also astronomical data spread to China[9].

---

[9] See Jastrow, *Religion* II 745 sq. and Boll, *Der ostasiatische Tierzyklus im Hellenismus* (Leiden 1912). I hope to treat this phase of the subject more fully in a special article. See for the present the summary of my paper on this subject in the Actes du IV[ère] Congrès International d'Histoire des Religions (Leiden 1913) 106-111 and Records of the Past (Washington) Vol. XII (1913) 12-16.

II

The observation of signs observed in young animals and in infants at the time of birth constitutes a third division of Babylonian-Assyrian divination, quite equal in prominence to Hepatoscopy and Astrology. Here too we are justified in seeking for some rational or quasi-rational basis for the importance attached by Babylonians and Assyrians, and as we shall see by other nations as well, to anything of a noteworthy or unusual character observed at the moment that a new life was ushered into the world. The mystery of life made as deep an impression upon primitive man and upon ancient peoples as it does on the modern scientist, who endeavors with his better equipment and enriched by the large experience of past ages, to penetrate to the very source of life. A new life issuing from another life—what could be stranger, what more puzzling, what more awe-inspiring? If we bear in mind that there is sufficient evidence to warrant us in saying that among peoples in a primitive state of culture, the new life was not associated with the sexual act[10], the mystery must have appeared still more profound. The child or the young animal was supposed to be due to the action of some spirit or demon that had found its way into the mother, just as death was supposed to be due to some malicious demon that had driven the spirit of life out of the body. The many birth customs found in all parts of the world[11], are associated with this impression of mystery made by the new life; they centre largely round the idea of protection to the mother and her offspring at a critical period. The rejoicing is tempered by the fear of the demons who were supposed to be lurking near to do mischief to the new life and to the one who brought it forth. The thought is a natural one, for the young life hangs in the balance, while that of the mother appears to be positively threatened. All bodily suffering and all

---

[10] See Hartland, *Primitive Paternity*—especially the summary in Chap. VII, and also Frazer, *Totemism and Exogamy* I 93 seq.; 191 seq. etc.
[11] See Ploß-Bartels, *Das Weib* (2ᵈ ed.) Chap. XXXII; *Das Kind* Chap. III, VIII, IX and Van Gennep, *Rites de Passage* Chap. V.

physical ailments being ascribed to the influence of bad demons, or to the equally malevolent influence of persons who could by their control of the demons or in some other way throw a spell over the individual, Birth, Puberty, Marriage and Death as the four periods in life which may be regarded as critical and transitional are marked by popular customs and religious rites that follow mankind from primitive times down to our own days. A modern scholar, Van Gennep, who has recently gathered these customs in a volume and interpreted them, calls his work 'Rites de Passage', i. e., customs associated with the four periods of transition from one stage to the other and which survive in advanced forms of faith as Baptism, Confirmation, Marriage ceremonies and Funeral rites, just as the chief festivals in all religions are the 'Rites de Passage' of nature—associated with the transition periods of the year, with the vernal equinox, the summer solstice, the autumnal equinox and the winter solstice or, expressed in agricultural terms, with sowing time, with blossoming or early harvest time, with the later harvest time and with the period of decay.

The significance attached to birth omens is thus merely a phase of the ceremonies attendant upon the passage of the new-born from its mysterious hiding place to the light. The analogy between the new life and the processes of nature is complete, for the plant, too, after being hidden in the earth, which is pictured in the religions of antiquity as a 'great mother', comes to the surface.

III

The field of observation in the case of the new-born among mankind and in the animal world is large—very large, and yet definitely bounded. Normal conditions were naturally without special significance, but any deviation from the normal was regarded as a sign calling for interpretation. Such deviations covered a wide and almost boundless range from peculiar formations of any part of the body or of the features, to actual malformations and monstrosities. The general underlying principle was, the greater the abnormality, the greater the significance attached to it; and as in the case of the movements in the heaven, the unusual was regarded as an indication of some imminent unusual occurrence. We are fortunate in possessing among the tablets of Ashurbanapal's library, unearthed by Layard just fifty years ago and which is still our main source for the Babylonian-Assyrian religious literature, many hundreds of texts furnishing lists of birth omens and their interpretation[12], just as we have many hundreds of texts dealing with liver divination[13], and even more dealing with Astrology[14], apart from the many hundreds of texts dealing with miscellaneous omens of which up to the present only a small proportion has been published[15]. From this division of the great collection gathered by Ashurbanapal's

---

[12] Part XXVII and Part XXVIII Pl. I-42 of *Cuneiform Texts from Babylonian Tablets etc. in the British Museum*, are taken up with texts of this character.

[13] Parts XX, XXX and XXXI and Pl. I-42 of Part XXVIII represent the bulk of this section of the Library so far as recovered by Layard, Rassam and George Smith. Previous to the British Museum publication, Alfred Boissier had published three volumes of divination texts of all kinds under the title of *Documents Assyriens relatifs aux Présages* (Paris 1894-99) and in his *Choix de Textes relatifs a la Divination Assyro-Babylonienne* (Paris 1905-06).

[14] The chief publications of astrological texts is by Ch. Virolleaud under the title *L'Astrologie Chaldéenne* (Paris 1903-13), consisting up to the present of four parts and two supplements containing texts, and four parts with two supplements containing the transliteration of these texts. Besides this publication, M. Virolleaud has published numerous fragments of texts in the periodical *Babyloniaca*, founded and edited by him. Cun. Texts, Part XXX Pl. 43-50 also contains astrological texts; Part XXXIII Pl. I-12 are aids to astrology.

[15] Chiefly by Boissier in the two works mentioned in note 2 on p. 6.

scribes chiefly from the temple archives of Babylonia, it appears that the bârû-priests made extensive collections of all kinds of omens which served the purpose of official hand-books to be consulted in case of questions put to the priests as to the significance of any particular phenomenon, and which were also used as textbooks for the training of the aspirants to the priesthood.

Confining ourselves to the birth-omens[16], the first question that arises is whether the signs entered are based on actual occurrences or are fanciful. In the case of many entries, as will presently be made evident, the anomalies noted rest upon actual observation, but with the desire of the priests to embrace in their collections all possible contingencies so as to be prepared for any question that might at any time arise, a large number of signs were entered which the diviners thought *might* occur. In other words, in order to be on the safe side the diviners allowed their fancy free rein and registered many things that we can positively say never did occur and never could occur[17]. With the help of hand-books on human and animal pathology, we can without difficulty distinguish between two classes. Thus, twins being regarded as significant and triplets even more so, the priests did not stop at this point but provided for cases when four, five six up to eight and more infants were born at one time[18]. Again in regard to

---

[16] Copious specimens of liver divinations texts in German translation with comments will be found in the author's *Religion Babyloniens und Assyriens* II 227-412; of Astrological Texts *ib* II 458-740; Oil and Water, Divination *ib* II 749-775; of Animal omens *ib* II 775-826; of Birth omens *ib* II 837-941 and a summary view of the miscellaneous omens *ib* II 946-969.

[17] The same is the case with the collections of liver signs and to a large extent also in the case of the astrological collections.

[18] Cun. Texts XXVII Pl. 24 Cases of more than three births at one time are extremely rare. A case of quintuplets in Groningen in the year 1897 is vouched for by Prof. Döderlein of Munich and one was reported in the newspapers recently as occurring in the United States. A case of sextuplets is noted by Vasalli in the Boll. Med. della Svizzera Italiana, 1894, Nos. 3 and 4. This seems to be the highest mark, though Pliny, Hist. Nat. VII 3, on the authority of Trogus records that a woman in Egypt gave birth to seven infants at one time; Lycosthenes, Prodigiorum ac. Ostentorum Chronicon

animals, inasmuch as bitches and sows may throw a litter of ten and even more, the priests in their collections carried the number up to thirty[19] which is, of course, out of the question. For sheep and goats the number was extended up to ten, though it probably never happened that more than triplets were ever born to an ewe or to a mother-goat. Even twins are rare, and I am told that there are few authenticated cases of triplets.

Malformations among infants and the young of animals were of course plentiful, but here too the anomalies and monstrosities are not as numerous and varied as were entered in the handbooks of the Babylonian and Assyrian diviners. The factor of fancy to which I have referred enters even more largely in the entries of many actual malformations, through the assumption of a more or less fanciful resemblance of some feature or of some part of an infant or of the young of an animal with the features or parts of some animal.

An excess number of limbs—three legs or four arms in the case of an infant, or five or six legs in the case of a lamb, puppy, pig or foal, or two heads—is not uncommon. On this basis the priests entered cases of excess legs and arms and heads up to nine and more[20]; and similarly in regard to ears and eyes.

That, however, despite the largely fanciful character of the entries in the omen texts, these collections not only rested on a firm basis of actual observation, but served a practical purpose is shown by the examples that we have of official reports made by the bârû-priests of human and animal anomalies, with the interpretations attached that represent quotations from the collections[21]. A report

---

(Basel 1557) p. 284 reports the same number born in the days of Algemundus, King of the Lombards.
[19] Cun. Texts XXVII Pl. 3.
[20] E. g. Cun. Texts XXVII Pl. 45 (K. 12050); XXVIII Pl. 42, 20.
[21] In the same way we have hundreds of *official* reports of occurences and observed phenomena in the heavens with the interpretations taken from the astrological texts; and we also have a large number of official reports of the same character dealing with the

of this kind in reference to an animal monstrosity reads in part as follows[22]:

'If it is a double foetus, but with one head, a double spine, two tails and one body, the land that is now ruled by two will be ruled by one person.

If it is a double foetus with one head, the land will be safe.'

We have here two quotations from a text furnishing all kinds of peculiarities connected with a double foetus and we are fortunate in having the text from which the quotations are made[23]. Evidently an ewe has given birth to a monstrosity such as is here described, the case has been reported to the diviners who furnish the king[24] with this report, indicating that since the monstrosity has only one head, what might have been an unfavorable omen is converted into a favorable one.

Another report [25]regarding a monstrosity born of a sow reads:

'If a foetus has eight feet and two tails, the ruler will acquire universal sway. A butcher, Uddanu by name, reported as follows: A sow gave birth (to a young) having eight feet and two tails. I

---

results of the inspection of the liver of a sacrificial animal, killed and inspected at a given time for the purpose of obtaining an answer to a question put. These reports are made in all cases to the rulers, which thus stamps them as official. See copious examples in Jastrow, *Religion*, II 227-271; 275-319 (Liver texts); 458-542; 578-584; 613-616; 639-652; 656-673; 688-692 (Astrological Texts).

[22] Cun. Texts XXVII Pl. 28.

[23] The first omen is taken from Cun. Texts XXVII Pl. 26, 11; the second from ib. line 10.

[24] The omens were always supposed to bear on events of a public import; hence the reports may always be assumed to be addressed to the reigning king, even when this is not expressly stated.

[25] Cun. Texts XXVII Pl. 45.

have preserved it in salt and kept it in the house. From Nergal-eṭir[26].'

Here we have the name of the bârû-priest who made the report expressly indicated. The report begins with a quotation from the collections, indicating the interpretation to be put upon the occurrence, after which the report of the actual event that took place is given in detail; and Nergal-eṭir is careful to add that he has preserved the specimen as a proof of its occurrence, precisely as to-day such a monstrosity would be bottled and kept in a pathological museum. In another report[27] containing various quotations from the collections of birth-omens and closing with one in regard to a mare that had given birth to two colts, one male and one female, with smooth hair over the ears, over the feet, mouth and hoofs, which is interpreted as a favorable sign[28], the one who makes the report adds 'Whether this is so, I shall ascertain. It will be investigated according to instructions'. Evidently, the facts had not been definitely ascertained and the diviner, while furnishing the interpretations for various possibilities, promises to inform himself definitely and report again as to the exact nature of the unusual occurrence. Frequently these omen reports contain interesting and important allusions to historical events which are then embodied in the collections[29]. In fact the event which followed upon any unusual or striking sign, whether in the heavens or among the newly born or what not, was carefully noted and on the principle of post hoc propter hoc was regarded as the event presaged by the sign in question. The definite indication of the interpretation to be put upon the omen itself was supplied by the actual event that followed upon the

---

[26] From other sources (cf. Jastrow, *Religion* II 467, 3) we know that Nergal-eṭir flourished during the reign of Esarhaddon, King of Assyria (705-668 B. C.).

[27] Cun. Texts XXXVII Pl. 30.

[28] The text from which this omen is quoted is found. Cun. Texts XXVII Pl. 48, 2-4.

[29] See examples in Jastrow, *Religion* II 227-244 (Sargon and Naram-Sin omens); 333 and 392 (murder of a ruler Urumu); 555, (invasion of Babylonia by Hittites); see also 226, 3; 843, 7 and articles by the writer in Zeitschr. f. Assyr. XXI 277-282 and Revue Sémitique XVII 87-96.

appearance of some sign, though it was not supposed that the sign would always be followed by the same occurrence. The point to which attention was primarily directed was whether the occurrence was of a favorable or an unfavorable nature. If favorable, the conclusion was drawn that the sign was a favorable one and hence in the event of its recurrence some favorable incident might be expected according to existing circumstances—victory in an impending battle, suppression of an uprising, recovery of some member of the royal household who may be lying ill, good crops at the approaching harvest or whatever the case may be—or in general a favorable answer to any question put by a ruler. The same would apply to a combination of signs, one of the fundamental principles of divination being—once favorable, always favorable.

Among the birth-omen reports we have one containing a historical reference of unusual interest[30].

'If the foetus is male and female—omen of Azag-Bau who ruled the land. The king's country will be seized.

If a foetus is male and female, without testicles, a son of the palace[31] will rule the land or will assert himself against the king.'

We must assume in this case that a monstrosity has been born, having partly male and partly female organs. The priest by way of interpretation notes a series of signs registered in the collections, all prognosticating an abnormal state of affairs—a woman on the throne, captivity, seizure of the throne by an usurper and revolt. We frequently find in the collections several interpretations registered in this way,—a valuable indication of the manner in

---

[30] Cun. Texts XXVII Pl. 6; also Boissier, *Documents Assyriens* 185 (the first publication of this text, the importance of which was recognized by Boissier) and Thompson, *Reports of the Magicians and Astrologers of Nineveh and Babylon* (London 1900) Nr. 276.

[31] I. e. A child of the harem—not the legitimate heir.

which these collections were compiled by the priests from a variety of documents before them. The name of this female ruler, hitherto known only from this report and from a list of proper names in which Azag-Bau occurred, has now turned up in an important list of early dynasties ruling in the Euphratean Valley, discovered and published by Scheil[32]. We may conclude, therefore, that at the time that Azag-Bau sat on the throne or shortly before, such a monstrosity actually came to light. As an unusual occurrence it presaged something unusual, and was naturally associated with the extraordinary circumstance of a woman mounting the throne. Azag-Bau according to the newly discovered list is the founder of a dynasty ruling in Erech as a centre and whose date appears to be somewhere between 2800 and 3000 B. C.—possibly even earlier. As a founder of a dynasty that overthrew a previous one, Azag-Bau must have engaged in hostilities with other centres, so that the second interpretation that 'the king's country will be seized' may well refer to some historical event of the same general period. Be that as it may, the important point for us is that we have here another proof of the practical purpose served by the observation of birth-omens.

---

[32] Les plus anciennes Dynasties connues de Sumer-Accad. Comptes Rendus de l'Acad. des Inscript. et Belles-Lettres 1911, 606-621.

IV

Passing now to some illustrations of birth-omens from the collections of the bârû-priests, let us first take up some texts dealing with omens from the young of animals. Naturally, the animals to which attention was directed were the domesticated ones—sheep, goats, cows, dogs, horses and pigs. Among these the most prominent is the sheep, corresponding to the significance attached to the sheep in liver divination where it is, in fact, the only animal whose liver is read as a means of forecasting the future[33]. As a result of this particularly prominent position taken by the sheep in birth-omens, the word isbu, designating the normal or abnormal foetus—human or animal—when introduced without further qualification generally indicates the foetus of a sheep[34].

A text[35] dealing with a double foetus, i. e., of a sheep[36], reads in part as follows:

'If it is a double foetus with slits (?) on the head and tail, the land will be secure.

If it is a double foetus and enclosed[37], confusion in the country, the dynasty [will come to an end].

If it is a double foetus, encompassed like an enclosure, the king will [subdue?] the land.

---

[33] The position occupied by the sheep in divination leads in astrology to the use of the Sumerian term Lu-Bat, i. e., 'dead sheep' as the designation of the planets, the association of ideas being 'dead sheep' == têrtu 'omen' and then == planet, because the planets were regarded as omens. In the larger sense, the moon and sun were included among the planets. See Jastrow, *Religion* II p. 448 sq. and the article "Sign and Name for Planets in Babylonian" quoted in note 1 on p. 1.

[34] See Jastrow *Religion* II 845, 1 and 847, 68.

[35] Cun. Texts XXVII Pl. 25-26 completed by the duplicate Pl. 27-28.

[36] Shown by the continuation of the text. Cun. Texts XXVII Pl. 26.

[37] I. e. twisted up in a heap.

If it is a double foetus and encompassed like an enclosure, confusion in the land, hostilities [in the country].

If it is a double foetus, encompassed like an enclosure, with slits on the body, end of the dynasty, confusion and disturbances in the country.

If it is a double foetus, encompassed like an enclosure, with twisted necks and only one head, the land will remain under one head.

***

If it is a double foetus, the heads enclosed, with eight legs and only one spine, the land will be visited by a destructive storm[38].

If it is a double foetus with only one head, the land will be secure, the ruler will prevail against his enemy, peace and prosperity in the country[39].

If it is a double foetus with one head, a double spine, eight feet, two necks and two tails, the king will enlarge his land.

If it is a double foetus with one head, double spine, two tails and one body, then the land that is ruled by two will be ruled by one.

If it is a double foetus with only one head and one spine, eight feet, two necks and two tails, the king will enlarge his land.

If it is a double foetus with only one neck, the ruler will enlarge his land.

---

[38] An interpretation evidently based on the fact of a destructive storm that swept over the land after the birth of a monstrosity as described in the omen.

[39] Three interpretations, gathered from various documents and here united.

If it is a double foetus with only one spine, the ruler will enlarge his land.

If it is a double foetus with only one mouth, the land will remain under the command of the king.

If it is a double foetus with only one breast, the land will be enlarged, rule of a legitimate king.

In order to grasp the principles underlying the interpretation of such omens, we must take as our starting point the conceptions connected with the various parts of the body. Bearing in mind that the omens deal primarily with public affairs and the general welfare and only to a limited extent with private and individual concerns[40], the head of the foetus by a natural association stands for the ruler or occasionally for the owner of the mother lamb. One head to the double foetus, therefore, indicates unity—a single rule—whereas two heads point to disruption of some kind. If the double foetus is so entwined as to be shut in within an enclosure, a similarly natural association of ideas would lead to the country being shut in, in a state of confusion, the land in a condition of subjugation or the like. On the other hand, if merely the heads are enclosed so as to give the impression of unity and the rest of the two bodies is disentangled, the unfavorable sign is converted into a favorable one. A second principle involved in the interpretation results in a more favorable conclusion if the double foetus shows less complications. So, a single neck or a single spine or a single breast or a single mouth point again, like a single head, towards unity and therefore to flourishing conditions in the land. In the case of legs and tails, to be sure, the conditions seem to be reversed—the eight legs and two tails and two necks with one

---

[40] Not infrequently a birth-omen is interpreted as applying to the owner of the mother lamb or to the household in which the lamb was born,—but generally as an alternative to an *official* interpretation bearing on public affairs. See e. g. below pp. 15 and 16.

head pointing to enlargement of the land, whereas a double foetus with only six or five feet forebodes some impending misfortune.

Let us proceed further with this text.

If it is a double foetus, one well formed and the second issuing from the mouth of the first[41], the king will be killed and his army will , his oil plantation and his dwelling will be destroyed[42].

If it is a double foetus, the second lying at the tail [of the first], with two breasts and two tails, there will be no unity in the land[43].

If it is a double foetus, and the second lies at the tail of the first and enclosed and both are living, ditto.

If it is a double foetus, and one rides over the other, victory, throne will support throne.

If it is a double foetus and one rides over the other and there is only one head, the power of the king will conquer the enemy's land.

If it is a double foetus, one above and one below, with only one spine and eight feet, four [Variant: 'two'] ears, and two tails, throne will support throne.

If it is a double foetus with the faces downward, approach of the son of the king, who will take the throne of his father, or a second son of the king will die, or a third son of the king will die.

✳✳✳

---

[41] I. e., lying at the mouth.
[42] I. e., presumably the plantation and house of the owner of the mother lamb.
[43] The opposite to this is 'throne will support throne', i. e., there will be mutual support.

If it is a double foetus with five feet, serious hostility in the country, the house of the man will perish, his stall[44] will be destroyed.

If it is a double foetus with six feet, the population will be diminished, confusion in the land.

If it is a foetus within a foetus, the king will weaken his enemy, his possessions will be brought into the palace[45].

❅❅❅

If a foetus gives birth to a second foetus[46], the king will assert himself against his opponent.

It will be observed that in quite a number of cases two alternative interpretations are given, one of an official character referring to the public welfare, or to occurrences in the royal household[47], the other of an unofficial character bearing on the welfare of the individual to whom the mother lamb that had produced the monstrosity belonged. One foetus issuing from the other, or one within the other, appears to have been a favorable or an unfavorable sign, according to the position of the second. If the one lay above the other, the association of ideas pointed to a control of the ruler over his enemy. In some cases, the association of ideas leading to the interpretation is not clear; and we must perhaps assume in such instances an entry of an event that actually occurred after the birth of the monstrosity in question. A certain measure of arbitrariness in the interpretations also constitutes a factor to be taken into consideration; and the last

---

[44] I. e., the stall of the owner of the mother lamb.
[45] I. e., the property of the owner of the mother lamb will be confiscated.
[46] I. e., the second issues from the belly of the other, or appears to do so.
[47] Whatever occurred to the king or to a member of his household was an omen for the *general* welfare under the ancient view of the king as the representative of the deity on earth.

thing that we need to expect in any system of divination is a consistent application of any principle whatsoever.

The text passes on to an enumeration of the case of an ewe giving birth to more than two lambs. The 'official' interpretations are throughout unfavorable[48], and the priests were quite safe in their entries which were purely arbitrary in these cases, since such multiple births never occurred. It is worth while to quote these interpretations as an illustration of the fanciful factor that, as already indicated, played a not insignificant part in the system unfolded.

If an ewe gives birth to three (lambs), the prosperity of the country will be annulled, but things will go well with the owner of the ewe, his stall will be enlarged.

If an ewe gives birth to three fully developed (lambs), the dynasty will meet with opposition, approach of an usurper, the country will be destroyed.

If an ewe gives birth to four, the land will encounter hostility, the produce of the land will be swept away, approach of an usurper, destruction in the land.

If an ewe gives birth to four fully developed lambs, [locusts (?)] will come and [destroy] the country.

If an ewe gives birth to four, approach of an usurper, the country will be destroyed.

If an ewe gives birth to five, destruction will ravage the country, the owner of the house will die, his stall will be destroyed.

---

[48] A partial exception, however occurs in the case of three and of ten lambs being produced at one birth. See below p. 18.

If an ewe gives birth to five, one with the head of a bull[49], one with a lion-head, one with a jackal-head, one with a dog-head and one with the head of a lamb[50], devastation will take place in the country.

If an ewe gives birth to six, confusion among the population.

If an ewe gives birth to seven,—three male and four female—, the king will perish.

If an ewe gives birth to eight, approach of an usurper, the tribute of the king will be withheld.

If an ewe gives birth to nine, end of the dynasty.

If an ewe gives birth to ten, a weakling will acquire universal sovereignty[51].

The general similarity of the interpretations may be taken as a further indication that the bârû-priests were simply giving their fancy free scope in making prognostications for conditions that could never arise; nor is it of serious moment that in the case of triplets the interpretation is favorable to the owner of the ewe, or that in the case of ten lambs, even the official interpretation is not distinctly unfavorable—in view of the purely 'academic' character of such entries.

An extract from a long text[52] furnishing omens derived from all kinds of peculiarities and abnormal phenomena noted on the ears of an animal—primarily again the sheep, though no doubt assumed to be applicable to other domesticated animals—will throw further light on the system of divination devised by the

---

[49] I. e., of course, the head resembles that of a bull.
[50] I. e., with a normal head.
[51] A variant reads, "the city will acquire sovereignty".
[52] Cun. Texts XXVII Pl. 37-38 of which again Pl. 36 is an extract.

bârû-priests, and will also illustrate the extravagant fancy of the priests in their endeavor to make their collections provide for all possible and indeed for many impossible contingencies.

If a foetus[53] lacks the right ear, the rule of the king will come to an end, his palace will be destroyed, overthrow of the elders of the city, the king will be without counsellors, confusion in the land, diminution of the cattle in the land, the enemy will acquire control[54].

If the foetus lacks a left ear, a god will harken to the prayer of the king, the king will take the land of his enemy, the palace of the enemy will be destroyed, the enemy will be without a counsellor, the cattle of the enemy's country will be diminished, the enemy will lose control.

If the right ear of the foetus is detached, the stall[55] will be destroyed.

If the left ear of the foetus is detached, the enemy's stall will be destroyed.

If the right ear of the foetus is split, the herd will be destroyed or the leaders of the city will leave (it)[56].

If the left ear of the foetus is split, the herd will be enlarged, the leaders of the enemy's country will leave (it).

---

[53] The term used throughout is isbu
[54] The unusual number of alternative interpretations—though all unfavorable—points to the compilation of the text from various sources in which the sign was again entered with a different interpretation in each. These varying interpretations are here united; and no doubt the priests felt that there was safety in numbers. One of the seven prognosticated events was quite certain to happen—at some time. The chief point was that the sign was unfavorable.
[55] I. e., the stall of the owner of the mother lamb.
[56] As above, an unofficial and an official interpretation.

If the right ear of the foetus is split and swollen with clay, the country [will have a rival].

If the left ear of the foetus is split and swollen with clay, the enemy's country will have a rival.

If the right ear of the foetus is destroyed, the stall will be enlarged, the stall of the enemy will be diminished.

If the outside of the right ear is destroyed, the land will yield to the enemy's land.

If the right ear of the foetus lies near the cheek[57], the enemy will prevail against the power of the king, the king will be without counsellors, a ruler will not inhabit the land, or the son of the king of universal sway[58] will be king.

If the left ear of the foetus lies near the cheek, an enemy will be installed in the royal palace.

If the right ear of the foetus lies near the jaw, birth of a demon[59] in my land, or in the house of the man[60].

If the left ear of the foetus lies near the jaw, birth of a demon in the enemy's land, or the land of the enemy will perish.

The guiding principle of the interpretation in these instances is the natural association of the right as your side and the left with the enemy's side. A defect on the right side is unfavorable to you, i. e., to the king or to the country or to the individual in whose household the birth occurs, while the same defect on the left side is unfavorable to the enemy and, therefore, favorable to you. The

---

[57] I. e., displaced.
[58] I. e., of Babylonia or Assyria.
[59] I. e., a demoniac being or a monstrosity of some kind.
[60] I. e., of the owner of the mother lamb.

principle is quite consistently carried out even to the point that if the sign itself is favorable, it is only when it is found on the right side that it is favorable to you, while its occurrence on the left side is favorable to the enemy.

Defects of any kind appear to be unfavorable, whereas an excess of organs and parts are in many instances favorable, though with a considerable measure of arbitrariness.

If the foetus has two ears on the right side and none on the left, the boundary city of the enemy will become subject to you.

If the foetus has two ears on the left side and none on the right, your boundary city will become subject to the enemy.

If the foetus has two ears on the right side and one on the left, the land will remain under the control of the ruler.

If the foetus has two ears on the left side and one on the right, the land will revolt.

If within the right ear of the foetus a second ear[61] appears, the ruler will have counsellors.

If within the left ear of the foetus there is a second ear, the counsellors of the ruler will advise evilly.

If behind the right ear of the foetus there is a second ear, the ruler will have counsellors.

If behind the left ear of the foetus there is a second ear, confusion in the land, the land will be destroyed[62].

---

[61] I. e., the rudiments of what seems to be a second ear.

✳✳✳

If a foetus has [four] ears, a king of universal sway will be in the land.

[If a foetus has four ears], two lying in front (and) two in back, the ruler will acquire possessions in a strange country[63].

✳✳✳

If behind the right ear, there are two ears, visible on the outside[64], the inhabitants of the boundary city will become subject to the enemy.

If behind the left ear there are two ears visible on the outside, the inhabitants of the boundary city of the enemy will become subject to you.

If a foetus has three ears, one on the left side and two on the right side, the angry gods will return to the country.

If a foetus has three ears, one on the left side and two on the right, the gods will kill within the country.

If within the right ear of a foetus there are three ears with the inner sides well formed, the opponent will conclude peace with the king whom he fears, the army of the ruler will dwell in peace with him.

---

[62] Similarly, a second ear appearing below or above (?) the other one, is a favorable sign; on the right side, therefore, favorable to you, on the left favorable to the enemy, and, therefore, unfavorable to your side.

[63] There is inserted at this point an omen for the case that "a foetus has eight (?) feet and two tails with unfavorable interpretations, approach of an usurper, no unity in the land, the land will destroy its inhabitants."

[64] I. e., not one within the other—in all, therefore, three ears.

If within the left ear of a foetus there are three ears with the inner sides well formed, thy ally will become hostile.

If behind each of the two ears there are three ears visible on the outside, confusion in the land, the counsel of the land will be discarded, one land after the other will revolt.

If within each of two ears there are three ears visible on the inner side, things will go well with the ruler's army.

If within each of the two ears there are three ears, visible on the outside and the inside, the army of the ruler will forsake him and his land will revolt.

If within each of the two ears there are three ears, visible on the outside and the inside, the army of the ruler will forsake him and his land will revolt.

If the ears of a foetus are choked up[65], in place of a large king a small king will be in the land.

In general, therefore, an excess number of ears points to enlargement, increased power, stability of the government and the like; and this is probably due in part to the association of wisdom and understanding with the ear in Babylonian[66], for as a general thing an excess of organs or of parts of the body is an unfavorable sign, because a deviation from the normal.

In the same way as in the case of the ears, we have birth-omen texts dealing with the head, lips, mouth, eyes, feet, joints, tail, genital organs, hair, horns and other parts of the body[67]. In many

---

[65] Literally "full".
[66] The 'wide-eared man' (rapaš uzni) is the wise man. Ashurbanapal in the subscript to the tablets of his library thanks the gods for having 'opened his ears wide', i. e. given him understanding etc.
[67] See the partial list of such texts, Jastrow, *Religion* II 851 note I.

of these texts dealing with all kinds of peculiar formations and abnormalities in the case of one organ or one part of the body or the other, a comparison is instituted between the features or parts of one animal with those of another and the interpretation is guided by the association of ideas with the animal compared. A moment's reflection will show the importance of this feature in extending the field of observation almost ad infinitum. A lamb born with a large head might suggest a lion, a small long head that of a dog, or a very broad face might suggest the features of a bull. From comparisons of this kind, the step would be a small one to calling a lamb with lion-like features, a lion, or a lamb with features recalling those of a dog, a dog and so on through the list, the interpretations being chosen through the ideas associated with the animal in question. A text of this kind[68], of which we have many, reads in part as follows.

If an ewe gives birth to a lion, the abandoned weapons will make an attack (again), the king will be without a rival.

If an ewe gives birth to a lion, but with a head of a 'rain bow' bird[69], the son will seize the throne of his father.

If an ewe gives birth to a lion, but (some of) the features are (also) human, the power of the king will conquer a powerful country.

If an ewe gives birth to a lion, but (some of) the features are those of a lamb, the young cattle will not prosper.

If an ewe gives birth to a lion, but (some of) the features are those of an ass, severe famine will occur in the country.

---

[68] Cun. Texts XXVII Pl. 21-22, with a duplicate Pl. 19 (K. 4132).

[69] For marratum "the rain-bow" see Jastrow, *Religion* II 739 note 7 and 875, note 3. The "rain-bow" bird must have been one distinguished by its manifold coloring. A lion-lamb with the head of a 'rainbow bird' was, therefore, a young lamb with a large lion-like head, but showing various hues and shades.

If an ewe gives birth to a lion, but (some of) the features are those of a dog, Nergal[70] will cause destruction.

If an ewe gives birth to a lion but (some of) the features are those of a khupipi[71], the ruler will be without a rival and will destroy the land of his enemy.

If an ewe gives birth to a lion, but with the mouth of a wild cow, the rule of the king will not prosper.

If an ewe gives birth to a lion but with the mouth of a bull, famine will ensue.

If an ewe gives birth to a lion with the horny exuberance of an ibex on its face, prices will be lowered[72].

If an ewe gives birth to a lion with the horny exuberance of an ibex on its face and if the eyes are open[73], prices will be high.

If an ewe gives birth to a lion with fatty flesh on the nose, the land will be well nourished.

If an ewe gives birth to a lion, and the right temple is covered with fatty flesh, the land will be richly blessed.

If an ewe gives birth to a lion, and the left temple is covered with fatty flesh,—rivalry.

If an ewe gives birth to a lion, and it is covered all over with fatty flesh, the king will be without a rival.

---

[70] The god of pestilence.

[71] An animal not yet identified.

[72] Low prices indicate hard times and are an unfavorable sign; high prices are favorable. The gods in ancient Babylonia and Assyria appear to have been on the side of the "Trusts".

[73] It is assumed that the abnormal birth is still-born, but in this particular case the eyes are open.

If an ewe gives birth to a lion but without a head[74], death of the ruler.

If an ewe gives birth to a lion with the gorge torn off[75], destruction of the land, the mistress[76] will die.

If an ewe gives birth to a lion with the gorge torn off and a mutilated tail[77], the land [will be destroyed (?)]

From texts like these it would appear that the phrase of 'an ewe giving birth to a lion' had acquired a purely conventional force to describe a lamb whose head or general features suggested those of a lion. It may have come to be used indeed for a newly born lamb of unusually large proportions. Hence one could combine with the description of a lion-lamb such further specifications as that it also suggested human features, or looked like an ass or a dog, or that while it came under the category of a lion-lamb, it yet had some of the features of a normal lamb. At all events we must not credit the Babylonians or Assyrians with so absurd a belief as that an ewe could actually produce a lion. Such a supposition is at once disposed of when we come to other texts where we find entries of an ewe producing a whole series of animals—a jackal, dog, fox, panther, hyena, gazelle, etc. and where we must perforce assume resemblances between a young lamb and the animals in question and not any extravagant views of possible cross-breeding[78]. To clinch the matter, we have quite a number of

---

[74] Such a monstrosity is known as Acephaly in modern nomenclature. See Kitt, *Lehrbuch der pathologischen Anatomie der Haustiere* (4 ed.) I, 72, for illustrations of an Acephalus bipes.

[75] Known in modern nomenclature as Brachyprosopy. See Kitt, ib. I 87 sq.

[76] Presumably the mistress of the household in which the monstrosity was born.

[77] Perokormy—See the illustration in Kitt, ib. I 75 sq.

[78] Cross-breeding, in fact, is a comparatively rare phenomenon in the animal world, limited to the horse and ass, horse and zebra, dog and wolf, dog and fox, or jackal, lion and tiger, ox and buffalo or yak, hare and rabbit, camel and dromedary, goat and mountain stag, and possibly lambs and goats. See Ellenberger-Scheunert, *Lehrbuch der vergleichenden Physiologie der Haussäugetiere* (Berlin 1910) 703.

passages in which the preposition 'like' is introduced[79] instead of the direct equation, showing that when the texts speak of an ewe giving birth to a lion, a jackal, a dog, etc., the priests had in mind merely a resemblance as the basis of such statements.

The general idea associated with the lion in divination texts is that of power, success, increase and the like. The sign, therefore, of an ewe producing a lion is a favorable one; it is only through attendant circumstances that the character of the sign is transformed into an unfavorable or partly unfavorable omen. So in case the lion-lamb has a head suggestive of the variegated colors of the rainbow bird, the sign still points to power, but to a power exercised by the crown prince against the father. If some of the features suggest those of an ass or of a dog or of a pig, the ideas associated with these animals convert what would otherwise have been a favorable sign into an unfavorable one. The mouth of a wild cow or of a bull, thus interfering with the complete identification of the young lamb as a lion-lamb, similarly, brings about an unfavorable interpretation. Fatty flesh by a natural association points to increased prosperity, while mutilations of the head, tail or of any other part naturally carry with them unfavorable prognostications.

It is interesting to see from a long list of comparisons of a new-born lamb with all kinds of animals[80] the extent to which the association of ideas connected with the animals in question is carried.

If an ewe gives birth to a dog ... the king's land will revolt.

---

[79] See the enumeration in Jastrow, *Religion* II 873 note 2, e. g., 'eyes like those of a dog' in the case of a newly-born lamb (Cun. Texts XVII Pl. 23, 14), 'foot like that of a lion' (Cun. Texts XXVII Pl. 45, 34), 'head like that of a dog' (Cun. Texts, XXVIII Pl. 36, 15); in the case of a double foetus 'both like a lion' or 'like a dog' (Cun. Texts XXVII Pl. 48, 11-12) etc.

[80] Cun. Texts XXVII Pl. 22, obv. 13-25.

If an ewe gives birth to a beaver[81] (?), the king's land will experience misery.

If an ewe gives birth to a fox, Enlil[82] will maintain the rule of the legitimate king for many years, or[83] the king will strengthen his power.

If an ewe gives birth to a Mukh-Dul[84], the enemy will carry away the inhabitants of the land, the land will despite its strength go to ruin, the dynasty will be opposed, confusion in the land.

If an ewe gives birth to a panther, the kingdom of the ruler will secure universal sway.

If an ewe gives birth to a hyena (?), approach of Elam.

If an ewe gives birth to a gazelle, the days of the ruler through the grace of the gods will be long, or the ruler will have warriors.

If an ewe gives birth to a hind, the son of the king will seize his father's throne, or the approach of Subartu will overthrow the land.

If an ewe gives birth to a roebuck, the son of the king will seize his father's throne, or destruction of cattle[85].

If an ewe gives birth to a wild cow, revolt will prevail in the land.

If an ewe gives birth to an ox, the weapons of the ruler will prevail over the weapons of the enemy.

---

[81] Ideographic designation 'water dog'.
[82] The chief god of Nippur and the older head of the pantheon.
[83] I. e., an alternative interpretation.
[84] An unidentified animal.
[85] I. e., an alternative interpretation of a less official character.

If an ewe gives birth to an ox that has *ganni*[86], the ruler will weaken the land of his enemy.

If an ewe gives birth to an ox with two tails, omen of Ishbi-Ura[87], who was without a rival.

If an ewe gives birth to a cow, the king will die, another king will draw nigh and divide the country.

One might have supposed that such omens represent a purely imaginative theoretical factor, but the introduction of the historical reference proves conclusively that the Babylonians and Assyrians attached an importance to the fancied resemblance of an animal to an other, and that in the case of such strange statements as that an ewe gives birth to one of a series of all kinds of animals, it is this fancied resemblance that forms the basis and the point of departure for the interpretation.

---

[86] See Jastrow, *Religion* II 879 note 9.
[87] Founder of the Isin dynasty (c. 2175 B. C.)—another illustration of an historical omen.

V

If, now, we turn to birth-omens in the case of infants, we find in the omen texts the same two classes, those in which all kinds of abnormalities and malformations are registered, and such in which the fancied resemblance of the new-born infant to some animal, or of some features of an infant to those of an animal is introduced as a factor. The principles underlying the interpretation, so far as they can be recognized, are naturally the same as in the case of birth-omens for the young of domesticated animals. A few illustrations will make this clear.

A text[88] dealing with twins, and passing on to multiple births up to eight, reads in part as follows:

If a woman gives birth to two boys, famine will prevail in the land, the interior of the country will witness misfortune, and misfortune will enter the house of their father[89].

If a woman gives birth to two boys with one body—no union between man and wife, [that house will be reduced][90].

If a woman gives birth to two boys of normal appearance, that house[91] ...

If a woman gives birth to a boy and a girl, ill luck will enter the land, the land will be diminished.

---

[88] Cun. Texts XXVII Pl. 4, 15-39, completed by the duplicates Pl. 3, 22-27 and Pl. 1, 1-2 and Pl. 6. The complete translation of the tablet with its various duplicates will be found in Jastrow, *Religion* II 900-916.
[89] An alternative 'unofficial' interpretation
[90] Two interpretations, both unofficial—a rather unusual case.
[91] The rest of the line is broken off.

If a woman gives birth to twins united at the spine, with the faces [back to back ?], the gods will forsake the country, the king and his son will abandon the city.

If a woman gives birth to twins without noses and feet, the land [will be diminished][92].

If a woman gives birth to twins in an abnormal condition, the land will perish, the house of the man will be destroyed.

If a woman gives birth to twins united at the sides[93], the land ruled by one will be controlled by two.

If a woman gives birth to twins united at the sides, (and) the right hand of the one lying to the right is missing, the weapon of the enemy will kill me, the land will be diminished, weakness will bring about defeat and my army will be destroyed.

If a woman gives birth to twins united at the sides, and the left hand of the one lying to the left is missing[94] ...

If a woman gives birth to twins united at the sides and the right hands are missing—attack, the enemy will destroy the produce of the land.

If a woman gives birth to twins united at the sides, and the left hands are missing, [the produce of the enemy's land will be destroyed][95].

---

[92] The line is defective, but the omen was without doubt unfavorable.
[93] As in the case of the famous Siamese twins.
[94] Interpretation broken off, but it was no doubt the reverse of what was entered in the preceding omen, i. e., unfavorable for the enemy and therefore, favorable to your side.
[95] The end of the line can be restored by comparison with the preceding omen.

If a woman gives birth to twins, united at the sides, and the right foot of the one lying to the right is missing, the enemy will abandon the rest of my land, the land will be captured.

If a woman gives birth to twins united at the sides, and the left foot of the one lying to the left, is missing, I will [abandon] the rest of the enemy's land, [and the land of the enemy will be captured[96]].

If a woman gives birth to twins united at the sides, and the right feet are missing, the seat of the country[97] will be overthrown and captured.

If a woman gives birth to twins united at the sides and the left feet are missing, the seat of the enemy's land [will be overthrown and captured].

If a woman gives birth to two girls, the house will be destroyed.

If a woman gives birth to two girls and they die[98] ...

If a woman gives birth to three well developed girls, the land of the ruler will be enlarged.

If a woman gives birth to two girls with one body, [no union] between man [and wife, the land will be diminished][99].

If a woman gives birth to two girls of normal appearance ...[100].

If a woman gives birth to three boys, distress will seize the land ...

---

[96] Restoration certain.
[97] I. e., the capital.
[98] Interpretation no doubt unfavorable.
[99] Restored by comparison with the second omen
[100] Rest of the line broken off, but the interpretation was no doubt unfavorable.

If a woman gives birth to [four (?)] boys, [destruction in the land][101].

Through another fragment[102], the list of multiple births is carried up to eight—a perfectly safe procedure on the part of the bârû-priests, since it is unlikely that the case of more than four births at one time ever occurred in the whole scope of Babylonian-Assyrian history. The interpretations in the case of more than triplets appear to have been consistently unfavorable. Even twins, as is apparent from the above entries, were generally regarded as unfavorable, because of the deviation from the normal involved; and this was certainly the case when monstrous factors were connected with the double birth—the two united at the backs or at the sides—or when the twins lacked a part of the body such as noses, hands or feet. The fundamental distinction between the right side as representing your side and the left as the enemy's side intervenes to differentiate between the application of the omen to the king or to the country on the one hand, and to the enemy or his country on the other.

Corresponding to the text above discussed, in which interpretations are offered for all kinds of malformations or peculiarities, in connection with the ears of newly-born animals, we have a text[103] furnishing omens in the same way in the case of human births.

If a woman gives birth, (and the child has) a lion's ear, a powerful king will rule in the land.

---

[101] The end of the line supplied by Cun. Texts XXVII Pl. 24, 16.
[102] Cun. Texts XXVII Pl. 241, 16 (K. 3881) to the close of the tablet.
[103] Cun. Texts XXVII Pl. 16, together with Pl. 17, 18—an extract from the fuller tablet.

If a woman gives birth, and the right ear[104] is missing, the life of the ruler will come to an end.

If a woman gives birth, and the left ear is missing, the life of the king will be long.

If a woman gives birth, and both ears are missing, famine will prevail in the country, and the land will be diminished.

If a woman gives birth, and the right ear is small, the house of the man will be destroyed.

If a woman gives birth, and the left ear is small, the house of the man will be enlarged.

If a woman gives birth, and both ears are small, the house of the man will be overthrown.

If a woman gives birth, and the right ear is detached[105], the house of the man will be destroyed.

If a woman gives birth, and the left ear is detached, the house of the opponent will be destroyed, the house of the man[106] will be enlarged.

If a woman gives birth, and both ears are detached, the house of the man will encounter misfortune.

If a woman gives birth, and the right ear reaches to the cheek, a weakling will be born in the man's house.

If a woman gives birth, and the left ear reaches to the cheek, a strong one will be born in the man's house[107].

---

[104] I. e., of the child; and so of course in every case.
[105] Compare the omen in the case of the young of an animal
[106] I. e., the father of the child.

If a woman gives birth, and both ears reach to the cheek, that land will be destroyed, protection will be withdrawn.

If a woman gives birth, and the right ear is deformed, a weakling will be born in the man's house.

If a woman gives birth, and the left ear is deformed, a strong one will be born in the man's house[108].

If a woman gives birth, and the right ear of the child lies at the lower jaw[109], the son of the man will destroy the man's house.

If a woman gives birth, and the left ear lies at the lower jaw, the son of the man will encircle the man's house[110].

If a woman gives birth, and there are two ears on the right side and the left ear is missing, the angry gods will return to the land and the land will have peace.

If a woman gives birth, and there are two ears on the left side and the right ear is missing, the counsel of the land will be disturbed.

***

If a woman gives birth, and both ears are flattened,—revolt.

The principle consistently applied throughout these omens is that a defect or deformity on the right side is an unfavorable sign, and that the same phenomenon on the left side is unfavorable to the enemy, or favorable to you. A large ear—suggesting that of a

---

[107] The 'left' side being unfavorable to the enemy is favorable to you. We may, however, expect to find in a variant text 'A weakling will be born in the enemy's house'.
[108] See preceding note.
[109] I. e., misplaced.
[110] I. e., protect it.

lion—points by association to enlargement and increased strength.

The text then passes on to other peculiarities.

If a woman gives birth, and (the child has) the mouth of a bird, that land will be destroyed.

If a woman gives birth, and the mouth is missing, the mistress of the house will die.

If a woman gives birth, and the right nostril is missing,—injury.

If a woman gives birth, and both nostrils are missing, the land will experience distress, the house of the man will be destroyed.

If a woman gives birth, and the jaws are missing[111], the days of the ruler will come to an end, the house will be destroyed.

If a woman gives birth, and the lower jaw is missing, the enemy will take the boundary strip of my land.

If a woman gives birth, and the arms (?) are missing, the house of the man will be destroyed.

If a woman gives birth, and the arms (?) are short, he will attain favor.

***

If a woman gives birth, and the upper lip rides over the lower one[112], he will attain favor.

---

[111] Agnathy in modern nomenclature. See Birnbaum, *Klinik der Mißbildungen* 73.
[112] I. e., the upper lip falls over the lower one.

If a woman gives birth, and the lips are missing, the land will encounter distress, the house of the man will be destroyed.

If a woman gives birth, and one arm is short, that man will be preferred[113].

If a woman gives birth, and the right hand is missing, that land will suffer destruction.

If a woman gives birth, and both hands are missing, the enemy will conquer the city of the new-born[114].

If a woman gives birth, and the fingers of the right hand are missing, the ruler will be hemmed in by his enemy.

If a woman gives birth, and there are six fingers on the right hand, misfortune will seize the house.

If a woman gives birth, and there are six toes on the right and on the left foot, the children[115] will encounter misfortune.

If a woman gives birth, and there are six toes on the right foot, there will be injury[116].

✵✵✵

If a woman gives birth, and the genital member is missing, the master of the house will be weakened, drying up of the field.

If a woman gives birth, and the genital member and the testicles are missing, the land will encounter misfortune, the woman[117] will suffer pain, the house[118] will control the palace[119].

---

[113] I. e., the father of the child
[114] I. e., the city in which the child was born.
[115] Of the same house.
[116] Presumably to the household in which the child was born.

If a woman gives birth, and the anus is closed[120], the land will suffer famine.

If a woman gives birth, and the anus [is missing ?], the king will be restrained in his palace.

If a woman gives birth, and the right thigh is missing, the land of the ruler will go to ruin.

If a woman gives birth, and the left thigh is missing, the enemy's land will go to ruin.

✳✳✳

If a woman gives birth, and both feet are missing, the course of the land will be checked, that house will be destroyed.

If a woman gives birth, and the right foot [of the child] is like that of a turtle[121], the enemy will destroy the property of the land.

If a woman gives birth, and hands and feet are like those of a turtle, the ruler will destroy the product of his land.

If a woman gives birth, and the feet are attached to the belly (?)[122], the possession of the house will be destroyed.

If a woman gives birth, and the child has only one foot, which is attached to the belly (?) and does not [touch] the ground[123] the land will suffer misfortune, the house will be destroyed.

---

[117] I. e., the mother.
[118] Variant 'the offspring', i. e., the newly born infant.
[119] I. e., there will be a political upheaval.
[120] This malformation of a child with a closed anus is frequently referred to in Roman omens, e. g., Julius Obsequens, de prodigiis (ed. Roßbach), §§ 26 and 40.
[121] I. e., only the rudiments of a foot are to be seen.
[122] I. e., they are directly attached to the body without thighs.

If a woman gives birth, and it has three feet of which two are entwined in one another[124] with the body, destruction will prevail in the land.

If a woman gives birth, and it has four feet and genital member and pudenda are there, the land will suffer misfortune, a strange ruler will appear on the scene.

If a woman gives birth, and the right leg is missing, the land of the ruler will go to ruin.

If a woman gives birth, and the left leg is missing, the enemy's land will go to ruin.

In general, malformations are looked upon as unfavorable, as are also excess organs or parts e. g. six fingers or six toes; and it is only occasionally that a peculiarity such as shortened arms or a protruding upper lip, receives a favorable interpretation. The variations in the interpretations themselves are not numerous, and for the most part are probably selected in an entirely arbitrary fashion, though here, too, as has been pointed out several times, association of ideas enters as a factor, as, e. g., where large ears are made to point to increased power. At the same time, it is also clear that the great majority of the malformations and abnormalities in the text that we have just discussed are such as actually do occur and with the help of medical works on human malformations[125], many of the omens described in this and in other texts can be identified. There can, therefore, be no doubt that the collections of the bârû-priests dealing with birth-omens observed in infants, likewise, rest upon actual observations, though the field was extended by passing on from actual to purely fanciful and impossible abnormalities. The extent to which this

---

[123] I. e., bent and deformed so that one cannot stand on it.
[124] Twisted legs as in the illustration in Jastrow's *Bildermappe zur Rel. Babyl. und Assyr.* No. 35.
[125] As, e. g., Guinard, *Précis de Teratologie* or Birnbaum, *Klinik der Mißbildungen.*

attempt to provide for all kinds of contingencies was carried in the collections is illustrated by a portion of the first tablet of a series[126] dealing with human birth-omens. This section treating in part of the birth of shapeless abortions reads as follows:

If a woman gives birth to pudenda[127], the royal dynasty will be changed.

If a woman gives birth to a head[128], the land will encounter distress.

If a woman gives birth to a form of some kind[129], king against king,—his rival, will prevail.

If a woman gives birth to a foetus[130], the land will encounter distress.

If a woman gives birth to a foetus in which there is a second, the rule of the king and of his sons will come to an end ... the power of the land [will dwindle].

If a woman gives birth to a mass of clay[131], the king's land will oppose him and cause terror.

If a woman is pregnant with a mass of clay and gives birth to a mass of clay, misfortune will come, the mother will close off her

---

[126] Cun. Texts XXVIII Pl. 34, with duplicate K 630 (Virolleaud, *Fragments des Textes Divinatoires* 9).
[127] I. e., a shapeless abortion suggesting pudenda.
[128] I. e., a miscarriage, shaped like a head.
[129] I. e., a shapeless mass.
[130] I. e., an embryo.
[131] I. e., a shapeless mass.

gate against the daughter, there will be no protection, the man[132] will go to ruin, the produce of the field will not prosper.

If a woman gives birth to a male still-birth, Nergal[133] will destroy, the man[134] will die before his time.

If a woman gives birth to a weak boy, distress, destruction of the house[135].

If a woman gives birth to a weak girl, that house will be destroyed by fire.

If a woman gives birth to a lame boy, distress, that house [will be destroyed].

If a woman gives birth to a lame girl, ditto.

If a woman gives birth to a cripple, that house will be plundered.

If a woman gives birth to a crippled girl, that house [will be destroyed ?].

☼☼☼

If a woman gives birth to something that has no face[136], the land will experience sorrow, that house will not prosper.

If a woman gives birth to a weakling, that city[137] [will experience misfortune ?].

---

[132] I. e., the father. Note the five alternative interpretations pointing again to the union of various collections of omens.
[133] The god of pestilence.
[134] I. e., the father of the child.
[135] In which the birth took place.
[136] Aprosopy.

If a woman gives birth to a crippled being, the land will experience sorrow, that house [will not prosper].

If a woman gives birth to a deaf mute, the house will be shut in.

***

If a woman gives birth to a dwarf[138] of a half-shape, that city will be opposed.

If a woman gives birth to a half-shaped being with bearded lips[139], talking[140], and that moves about, and has teeth[141]—hostility of Nergal, the crushing force of a powerful attack on the land, a god[142] will destroy, streets will be attacked, houses will be seized.

One may question whether all of such monstrosities actually occurred, though they are all possible, if we add the factor of fancy to account for some of the descriptions. The conventional character of the interpretations and the constant repetition of the same prognostications likewise indicate the desire on the part of the bârû-priests to exhaust their medical knowledge of monstrosities and malformations that could occur, in order to swell the collections to the largest possible proportions. The first

---

[137] In which the birth took place.

[138] The expression used is tigri ili 'a divine tigru'—which I take to be the Babylonian term for dwarf. See Jastrow, *Religion* II 913 note 7.

[139] Elsewhere we find the anomaly of a child born with a beard or with hair on the chin referred to. See Jastrow, *Religion* II 929.

[140] The talking infant (see also Jastrow, *Religion* II 929 note 6) occurs frequently as a prodigy in Roman literature. See Lycosthenes, Prodigiorum ac Ostentorum Chronicon 113. 228 etc.

[141] See further Jastrow, *Religion* II 928—infants born with one tooth, with two teeth or a number of teeth. The omen is also found in Roman literature, Livy, Historia XLI, 21; Pliny, Hist. Nat. VII, 15. King Richard the Third is among the historical personages said to have been born with teeth and which was regarded as an evil omen. (See Henry V, 3d Part. Act V, 6. 53 and 75.)

[142] Nergal, the god of pestilence, is meant. The text adds as a note 'Such a being is called a divine tigru'. See note 1 above.

tablet of the series[143] of which an extract has just been given, begins with an enumeration of various animals to which a newly born infant bears a resemblance and which is expressed, similarly to what we found in the animal birth-omens, by the phrase that the woman gives birth to the animal in question. The series begins as follows:

If a woman gives birth, and the offspring cries in the womb, the land will encounter sickness.

If a woman gives birth, and the offspring cries in the womb and it is distinctly heard, a powerful enemy will arise and overthrow the land, destruction will sweep the land, the enemy will destroy the precious possession, or the master's house will be destroyed.

If a woman gives birth to a lion, that city will be taken, the king will be captured.

If a woman gives birth to a dog, the master of the house will die and that house will be destroyed, confusion, Nergal will destroy.

If a woman gives birth to a pig, a woman will seize the throne.

If a woman gives birth to an ox, the king of universal rule will prevail in the land.

If a woman gives birth to an ass, the king of universal rule will prevail in the land.

If a woman gives birth to a lamb, the ruler will be without a rival.

If a woman gives birth to a Sâ[144], the ruler will be without a rival.

---

[143] Cun. Texts XXVI Pl. 4 with various duplicates and 'extract' tablets. See Jastrow, *Religion* II 907, note 1.
[144] An unidentified animal.

If a woman gives birth to a serpent[145], I will surround the house of the master.

If a woman gives birth to a dolphin (?)[146], the house of the [man will be enlarged ?].

If a woman gives birth to a fish-being[147], the rule of the king will prosper, the gods [will return to the land].

If a woman gives birth to a bird[148],...

These examples will suffice to show the part played by the supposed resemblance of a new-born infant with one animal or the other in the Babylonian-Assyrian birth-omens; nor is it difficult to see how the thought of such resemblances should arise, for, as a matter of fact, the shape of the head of an infant easily suggests that of a dog or a bird. The ear if unusually large might recall a donkey's ear; a small eye, that of a pig, and a large one, that of a lion[149]. The association of ideas with the various animals no doubt suggests the interpretation in most cases, though in others the interpretation appears to be of a purely conventional type and as a rule favorable.

---

[145] In another list of birth-omens a woman giving birth to a serpent is interpreted that 'the king will increase in power' (Cun. Texts XXVIII Pl. 43, 9).

[146] Alluttu—described elsewhere (Cun. Texts XXVIII Pl. 46, 9), as a fish with a thick head—probably, therefore, a dolphin.

[147] Such a malformation with the feet united and ending in the rudiments of toes that resemble fish's tail is still called a 'Sirenformation' in modern nomenclature. See Guinard, *Précis de Teratologie* 366 with illustrations fig. 178 and 179. See also Lycosthenes l. c. 142 and 316, also Hirst and Piersol, Human Monstrosities 88 and Pl. VII (sireno-melus).

[148] The interpretation is broken off.

[149] Cun. Texts XXVIII Pl. 3, 10; where this comparison is introduced with the interpretation that 'the king will be without a rival'.

VI

Now what does all this mean? Is there any larger significance in these elaborate collections of birth-omens? Do investigations of this character serve any purpose beyond finding out how foolish many millions of people were thousands of years ago, though to be sure it may be some satisfaction to ascertain for oneself that foolishness has so venerable an ancestry. Bouché-Leclercq says at the close of his introduction to his great work on Greek Astrology[150] that 'it is not a waste of time to find out how other peoples wasted theirs'. But there would be small comfort even in such a reflection, if studies in the history of divination did not furnish a larger outlook on the development of human thought—if in short such studies did not have some important bearing on the cultural history of mankind. Let us see whether this is the case.

Such is the curious nature of man that his science starts with superstition. The intellectual effort involved in developing what to us at least must appear as a foolish and erroneous notion, nevertheless, results in some positive advantage. We often hear it said that medicine starts with religion, and this is true in the sense that the cure of disease was once closely bound up with the belief that all suffering was due to some demon or invisible spirit that had entered the body—a view that is after all not so far removed from the modern 'germ' theory holding for so many diseases, for the germs are practically invisible and their demoniac character will assuredly not be denied. The cure of a disease in primitive medicine consisted in driving the demon out of the body, for which again we might without much difficulty find an equivalent in modern medicinal methods. Incantations were supposed to have the power of frightening the demon or in some other way of inducing them to leave the body of the victim, but it was soon discovered that certain herbs and concoctions helped to this

---

[150] *L'astrologie Grecque* IX.

end—not that it was at first supposed that such herbs and concoctions were useful to the patient, but that they were obnoxious to the demons who preferred to leave their victims rather than endure the nasty and ill-smelling combinations that frequently form the medical prescriptions attached to the incantations[151]. What we would regard as medicinal remedies were originally given to the patient, with a view and in the hope of disgusting the demon that had caused the disease—a supplement therefore to the power attributed to the recitation of certain combinations of words, and all with a view to force the demons to release their hold on the sufferer by quitting his body. From such superstitious beginnings medicine, closely bound up with the prevailing religious beliefs, took its rise. In the same way, liver divination though as a practice it belongs to the period of primitive culture and rests on an asumption which from the modern scientific point of view is the height of absurdity, nevertheless, led to the study of anatomy and as a matter of fact, the observation of the liver for purposes of divination represents the beginnings of the study of anatomy[152]. Astrology led to astronomy, and in the same way the observation of birth-omens gave rise to another science or at least to a mental discipline that until quite recently was regarded as a science—namely, the study of human and animal physiognomy. The importance given to any and to all kinds of peculiarities in the case of the young of animals and in new-born infants naturally sharpened the powers of observation, and led people to carefully scrutinize and study the features of the new-born. The large part played in this scrutiny by the supposed resemblance of the features of an infant to those of some animal formed a natural starting point, from which it was not a very large step to the position that this supposed resemblance had a bearing on the child itself. In other words the birth-omens in so far as they referred to phenomena among infants had a double significance; they portended

---

[151] See numerous examples in Cun. Texts XXIII.
[152] See the writer's paper on 'The Liver and the Beginnings of Anatomy' quoted on p. I note I.

something of moment either to the general welfare or to the house in which the birth took place and also to the child.

It is certainly not accidental that in the study of Human Physiognomy as carried on among the Greeks and Romans as well as among mediaeval Arabic and Christian writers, the supposed resemblances of people to animals was one of the chief methods employed for determining the character of an individual. This phase of Human Physiognomy I venture to trace back directly to divination through birth-omens, which would by a natural process lead to the study of human features as a means of ascertaining the character of an individual. Among the Greeks, the great Plato[153] was supposed to approve of the theory that a man possesses to some extent the traits of the animal that he resembles; and it seems to be a kind of poetic justice that a philosopher holding so manifestly absurd a theory should himself, as will presently appear, have been compared by a celebrated physiognomist of the 16th century to a dog—though to be sure to a dog of the finer type. Polemon and Adamantius many centuries after Plato are among the significant names of those who tried to work out the theory in the form of an elaborate science[154]. Aristotle who can generally be counted upon to have sane views on most subjects opposed this method of studying human character, though until a few decades ago a work on Human Physiognomy[155] based on the theory of a man's possessing the traits of the animal that he resembles passed as a production of Aristotle. It is one of the many merits of modern scholarship to have removed this stigma from the prince of Greek philosophers.

---

[153] On the basis of such passages as Phaedo, § 31.
[154] See Scriptores Physiognomici Graeci et Latini (ed. Richard Foerster, Leipzig 1903, 2 vols.) containing the treatises of Pseudo-Aristotle, Polemon, Adamantius and others. See Chapter I of Polemon (ed. Foerster I 108) and Chapter II (170-198); Chapter II, 2 of Adamantius (349 sq.) for a long enumeration of the resemblances between man and animals and the conclusions to be drawn therefrom.
[155] 'Physiognomika' included in Foerster's edition I 5-91. See Foerster's Prolegomena to his edition XIX, 2.

Aristotle, as a matter of fact, in a significant passage in his de Generatione Animalium (IV, 54) denies the possibility of the crossing of an animal of one species with that of another, and adds that malformations can produce apparent similarities between animals of different species, but which are to be explained through the workings of natural laws. These laws condition deviations from the normal as well as all normal phenomena. Nothing in nature, Aristotle sums up, can be contra naturam. It would appear from passages like this that in Aristotle's days the resemblances between an animal of one species and that of another, and the resemblance between man and animals had led to the belief of cross breeds to account for such resemblances, while monstrosities among animals and among men were looked upon as omens sent by the gods as a warning or as curses for crimes committed—a point of view that, as we shall see, is likewise to be traced back to Babylonian-Assyrian influences.

There were others besides Aristotle who opposed the current views, but the curious thing is that even those who rejected the theory of a transition of one species to another still maintained that certain traits in an individual could be associated with and explained by features that they had in common with some animal or the other. Notable among these was Giovanni Porta, a most distinguished scholar of the 16th century, who while a believer in magic was also a scientific investigator whose researches proved of great value in developing a true theory of light and who among other achievements invented the camera obscura. He wrote a work in Latin, de Humana Physiognomica (Sorrento, 1586) which he himself translated into Italian (Naples, 1598) and which subsequently appeared in French and German editions. It remained in fact the standard work on the subject up to the time of Lavater's great work on Physiognomy at the end of the 18th century. Porta opposed Plato's theory that a man has the traits of the animal that he resembles, on the ground that a man may have features suggesting various animals. His forehead may recall that of a dog, while his mouth may be like the snout of a swine, and his ears may resemble those of an ass. In fact Porta maintains that no man has features all of which suggest a comparison with one animal only. Yet Porta is of the opinion that the resemblance between men and animals, which is self-evident, forms the basis for the study of human character, with this modification, however, which makes the theory even more complicated, that each feature,—the forehead, the eyes, the nose, the mouth, the ears, the lips and even the eyebrows, and the color of hair of the head or the beard—betrays some characteristic. It is through the combination of all these features that the character is to be determined, but each feature is compared by Porta to the corresponding one of some animal and its significance set forth according to the idea associated with the animal. Porta's treatise is, therefore, quite as largely taken up with comparisons between men and animals as are the treaties of other Physiognomists, only in more detailed fashion. Thus a long forehead or one not too flat or too even, suggested to Porta the character of a sagacious dog and by way of illustration [156] places the portrait of a dog side by side with one traditionally supposed to be a likeness of Plato. Dante, so Porta tells us, also had such a dog forehead. A square forehead suggests that of a lion (115) and points to magnanimity, courage and prudence—provided, he adds, the rest of the face is in proportion; a high, rounded forehead (117) is compared with that of an ass, and is an indication of stupidity and imprudence. In the case of noses, comparisons are instituted with the beaks of ravens, eagles and roosters, with the noses of oxen, swine, dogs, apes and stags, and horses. Since the raven is an impudent and rapacious bird, he who is endowed by nature with a nose that curves from the forehead outward will also show these unpleasant qualities; on the other hand, if the nose is shaped like an eagle's beak, the person will share the magnanimity and royal spirit of the bird of Jupiter. The illustration (150) shows the picture of the Emperor Sergius Galba, side by side with an eagle's face. Cyrus and Artaxerxes, too, are said to have had noses of this

---

[156] I quote from the Latin ed. of 1593 (Hanovia).

fortunate shape; and by way of confirmation of the theory, Porta gives illustrations of the magnanimity of these and of other rulers who had a beak like that of an eagle. A nose broad in the middle and sloping inwards (154), suggesting that of an ox, indicates a lying and verbose individual; a thick nose (155) is pictured side by side with a swine's head with the usual uncomplimentary traits associated with that animal. In this way and in most detailed fashion Porta takes up in succession the mouth, the ears, the eyes, the teeth, the lips, the hair and the face in general[157]. A very large and broad face is compared with that of an ox or ass (172 seq.) and indicates ignorance, stupidity, laziness and obstinacy; a very small face resembles that of a cat or an ape (174 seq.) and prognosticates timidity, shrewd servility and narrowness; a very fleshy face is again compared with that of an ox (177); a very bony one with that of an ass, though Porta here as elsewhere is somewhat embarrassed by the variant opinions of his authorities Pseudo-Aristotle, Polemon and Adamantius and not infrequently has recourse to textual changes in order to solve difficulties. The doubt as to the reasonableness of the whole theory never appears, however, to have entered his mind, and he cheerfully proceeds with his comparisons in the course of which he introduces notable historical personages as illustrations. In this way Socrates is compared to a stag and because of his baldness is given a malignant, and, according to others, a lascivious nature (87); the Emperor Vitellius is likened to an owl (12); Actiolinus to a hunting dog because of the groove above his eyes (125); Plato, as we have seen, to a dog and Sergius Galba to an eagle, while the head of Alexander the Great, though only of medium size, is compared with that of a lion (72).

Such was the influence of Porta's work that it remained the authority for the study of Human Physiognomy till towards the

---

[157] He also has a series of chapters on the voice, which are much more reasonable in character because of the omission of any comparisons with animals; and passes on to the hands, the breast, the belly and the thighs and feet, and the general shape of the body.

end of the 18th century when Lavater's four volumes of "Physiognomical Fragments"[158] appeared with their wonderful illustrations, to which the profound impression made by the work was largely due. Lavater constantly refers to Porta, but one of his main objects is to controvert the thesis that the comparison of human features with those of animals should form the means of determining the trait indicated by the feature in question. Curiously enough in a preliminary outline of his system of Physiognomy[159], Lavater had included a chapter on the resemblance between man and animals, but by the time he came to work out his system he had changed his mind and henceforth opposed Porta's view. To be sure, the grounds on which he does so are more of a sentimental than of a scientific character. Lavater—a clergyman and a believer in the special creation of man by the Divine Power (Physiognomische Fragmente II 192),—protests against a possible relationship between man and the animal world, declaring that to see animal features in the human face is to lower the dignity of mankind. Man created as God's supreme achievement can have nothing to do with the animal creation which represents a lower order of being. Even Lavater does not go so far as to deny all resemblances between human features and those of animals. He admits and sympathizes and enlarges on them in several passages (II 192; IV 56); but he ascribes them to accident or to fancy, and declines to draw therefrom the conclusion that the individual who has some feature or a number of features that suggest those of some animal must, therefore, have the traits associated with the animal or the animals in question. It is rather strange that Lavater should not have hit upon the real objection to Porta's method which lies in the contradictions in which he necessarily involves himself by comparing the various features of an individual with various animals, the forehead with one animal, the eyes with another, the lips with a third and so on; and since the animals in question show entirely different and contradictory traits, it is manifestly

---

[158] *Physiognomische Fragmente* (Leipzig 1775-1778).
[159] *Von der Physiognomik* (Leipzig 1772), 2. Stück p. 45.

impossible to reach any rational conclusions as to a man's character by so absurd a method. However, although Lavater does not reveal the real weakness of the current theory of Human Physiognomy, yet he contributed to the overthrow of the theory itself which had reached the stage of reductio ad absurdum through the modifications introduced by Porta. It often happens that an outlived theory is set aside through arguments that are in themselves insufficient to do so.

Through Lavater the study of Physiognomy was thrown back on the scrutiny of human features, and the determination of a man's character by a direct method and without recourse to comparisons with the features of animals. In thus removing, however, what had been one of the props of the study of Human Physiognomy, Lavater shook the foundation of the study itself. With the advent of modern medicine, the study of Physiognomy was dethroned from the place that it had so long occupied and was relegated to the pseudo-sciences—an interesting and in many respects a suggestive intellectual discipline, but not a science. As a recent writer tersely puts it 'The physiognomical feeling and sensation will never die out among people, for the roots lie deep in human nature. It is erroneous, however, to attempt to construct a science out of it'[160].

The thought, however, of endeavoring to determine the character of an individual by a study of the peculiarities and striking indications of his features would never have arisen, but for the antecedent beliefs that gave to the observation of birth-omens so prominent a place among methods of divination. Corresponding to the emphasis laid upon the individual factor when Babylonian-Assyrian Astrology passed to the Greeks and which led to 'Genethlialogy' or the casting of the individual horoscope as the chief phase of astrology, in contradistinction to the exclusive

---

[160] Fritz Neubert, *Die volkstümlichen Anschauungen über Physiognomik in Frankreich bis zum Ausgang des Mittelalters* (Munich Dissertation 1910) 118.

bearing of astrology in its native haunt on the general welfare[161], the Babylonian-Assyrian system of divination through the study of birth-omens received an individualistic aspect upon passing to the Greeks and Romans, by leading to the study of human features as a means of determining the character of an individual; and with the character also the prognostication of the fate in store for him during his earthly career. In other words, the rise of the study of Human Physiognomy finds a natural explanation, if we assume that it takes its rise from a system of divination based on the observation of peculiarities noted at the time of birth. It was natural when divination methods were employed to forecast the future of the individual, that the thought should arise of a close relationship between the features of an individual and his personality, which would include the powers and qualities bestowed on him, and which determine his actions and the experiences he will encounter. The fact that in this pseudo-science of Physiognomy, the comparison between man and animals played so significant a part among Greek and Roman Physiognomists and through them among the scientists of Europe till almost to the threshold of the modern movement in science, adds an additional force to the thesis here set forth. Such a method of determining the traits possessed by an individual, and which was the keynote of Human Physiognomy till the days of Lavater, would not have maintained so strong a hold on thinkers and on the masses had it arisen in connection with the study itself. It was embodied into the study of Human Physiognomy as an integral part of it, because it represented an established tradition. The Babylonian-Assyrian birth-omens in which this very comparison between man and animals forms so important a factor furnish the natural conditions for the rise of the tradition, while the long range of time covered by the Babylonian-Assyrian birth-omens supply the second factor needed to account for the persistency of the tradition after it had passed beyond the confines within which it arose.

---

[161] See Jastrow *Religion*, II 704 sq.

VII

Now in order to justify the proposition that the study of Human Physiognomy, as developed among the Greeks and Romans and as passed on to others with its insistence on the fancied resemblance between man and animals as a leading and indeed as a fundamental factor, is to be directly carried back to the birth-omens of Babylonia and Assyria, we ought to be able to establish that among Greeks and Romans the abnormalities observed at the birth of infants and of the young of animals were really regarded as omens, and that such omens show a sufficient affinity to what we find among Babylonians and Assyrians to warrant the conclusion that, just as Hepatoscopy and Astrology came to the Greeks and Romans through influences emanating from the Euphrates Valley, so also the third large division of divination methods may be traced to the same source. Let us first take up the Romans for which the material at our disposal is so much more abundant.

Julius Obsequens, a writer whose exact date has not yet been determined, collected in his famous Liber de Prodigiis[162] all the omens that had been noted during a certain period of Roman history. He enumerates in all 72 covering the years 55 to 132 A. D. and the list itself is an instructive commentary on the attention that was paid to 'signs' of all kinds among the Romans as an index of the will and the intention of the gods. We find references to such phenomena as a rain of stones,—presumably hail stones—of oil, blood and milk—apparently allusions to volcanic eruptions, disguised in somewhat fanciful language—of the sun seen at night—perhaps a description of an eclipse when to a frightened populace it might appear as though night had suddenly set in—of blood appearing in rivers and of milk in lakes—no doubt a pollution of some kind due perhaps to masses of earth or to glacial deposits pouring into the river—to burning

---

[162] I quote Rossbach's edition in the Teubner Series.

torches in the heavens—probably comets with long tails—and more the like, all indicative of the unbridled play of popular fancy and showing that among the Romans, as among Babylonians and Assyrians, all unusual occurrences were looked upon as omens—portending some unusual happenings. Now among the 72 signs of Julius Obsequens there are quite a number of actual birth-omens, the character of which is so close to what we find in the collections of the bârû priests as to show a practical identity in the points of view. So we are told of several instances of a mule (supposed to be sterile) giving birth to a young (§ 65), in one case even to triplets (§ 15), in another to a young with five feet (§ 27). For the year 83 he records among various remarkable occurrences all regarded as omens, the birth of a colt with five feet (§ 24); two years in succession a two-headed calf (§ 31-32). Very much as in the Babylonian-Assyrian collections we read (§ 14) of a sow giving birth to a young with the hands and feet of a man. Among human monstrosities, our author records the case of a boy with three feet and one hand (§ 20), with one hand (§ 52), a boy with a closed anus (§ 26, 40), with four feet, four eyes and four ears and with double genital members (§ 25). Several instances are given of androgynous infants (§ 22, 32 and 36). Twins born at Nursia in the year 100 are described as follows, 'the girl with all parts intact, the boy with the upper part of the belly open, revealing the intestines[163], the anus closed, and speaking as he expired' (§ 40). The talking infant is a not infrequent phenomenon. In the following year the birth of a boy who said 'ave' is recorded (§ 41). Again, as in the collections of the bârû priests, we read (§ 57) of a woman giving birth to a serpent.

To these birth-omens further examples can be added from that inexhaustible storehouse of encyclopaedic knowledge, the Natural History of Pliny the Younger who, among other things, tells us

---

[163] In the Babylonian-Assyrian birth-omens, such cases, expressed by the phrase 'middle portion open', are very frequent, e. g., Cun. Text XXVII Pl. 44 (K 3166); 47, 14-15; 44 etc.

(Hist. Nat. VII 3) of a woman Alcippa who gave birth to a child with the head of an elephant[164]. Valerius Maximus in his de Dictis Factisque Memorabilibus devotes a chapter to Prodigia[165] of the same miscellaneous character as the collection of Julius Obsequens—many in fact identical—among which by the side of rivers flowing with blood, talking oxen who utter words of warning[166], rain of stones, mysterious voices, we also find birth-omens such as the speaking infant and the child with an elephant's head[167]. Suetonius[168] tells us that Caesar's horse had human feet and that the Haruspices—the Etruscan augurs—declared it to be an omen that the world would one day belong to Caesar. We see, therefore, that among the Romans birth-omens were regarded from the same point of view as among the Babylonians and Assyrians and that the interpretation of the omens was the concern of a special class who acted as diviners. Now the question may properly be put at this juncture, whether we are in a position to trace the actual interpretation of birth-omens among the Romans back to the Babylonian-Assyrian bârû-priests? To this question, I think an affirmative answer may unhesitatingly be given. We have in the first place the testimony of Cicero[169], as well as other writers[170] that the Etruscans who are described as skilled in all kinds of divination were especially versed in the interpretation of malformations among infants and among the young of animals. Cicero emphasizes more particularly by the side of birth-omens, divination through the sacrificial animal and through phenomenen in the heavens, thus giving us the same three classes that we find among Babylonians and

---

[164] In the same paragraph he records the birth of a serpent by a woman as in Julius Obsequens § 57.
[165] Book I, 6.
[166] E. g., cave tibi, Roma (I, 6, 5) at the time of the Second Punic War.
[167] I, 6, 5. Further examples of all kinds of omens are found in Chap. 8 of the first book of the Memorabilia.
[168] Life of Julius Caesar § 61.
[169] De Divinatione I 41-42.
[170] Arnobius, Adversum Nationes VII 26 calls Etruria the genetrix et mater superstitionis.

Assyrians. Since Hepatoscopy and Astrology among Greeks and Romans can be traced back directly to Babylonia and Assyria, the presumption is in favor of the thesis that the Etruscan augurs derived their birth-omens also from the same source. The character of the specimens that we have of the Etruscan interpretations of birth-omens strengthens this presumption. So, e. g., Cicero preserves the wording of such a birth-omen[171] which presents a perfect parallel to what we find in the collections of the Babylonian-Assyrian bârû priests, to wit, that if a woman gives birth to a lion, it is an indication that the state will be vanquished by an enemy. If we compare with this a statement in a Babylonian-Assyrian text dealing with birth-omens[172], vis.:

'If a woman gives birth to a lion, that city will be taken, the king will be imprisoned',

it will be admitted that the coincidence is too close to be accidental. The phraseology, resting upon the resemblance between man and animals, is identical. The comparison of an infant to a lion, as of a new-born lamb to a lion is characteristic of the Babylonian-Assyrian divination texts and even the form of the omen, stating that the woman actually gave birth to a lion is the same in both while the basis of interpretation—the lion pointing to an exercise of strength—is likewise identical. Ordinarily the resemblance of the feature of an infant to that of a lion points to increased power on the part of the king of the country, but in the specific case, the omen is unfavorable also in the Babylonian text. It is the enemy who will develop power, so that the agreement between the Babylonian and Etruscan omen extends even to the exceptional character of the interpretation in this particular instance.

---

[171] De Divinatione I 53.
[172] Cun. Texts XXIII Pl. 14, 4.

In the same passage¹⁷³, Cicero refers to the two-fold interpretation given for the case of a girl born with two heads, one that there will be revolt among the people, the other that the marriage tie will be broken. We thus have two interpretations, one bearing on the public weal, the other on private affairs, corresponding to the frequent combination of 'official' and 'unofficial' interpretations in the collections of the bârû-priests¹⁷⁴. The specific interpretations are again of the same character as we find in the Babylonian-Assyrian texts, 'revolt'¹⁷⁵ being in fact one of the most common, while the other corresponds to the phrase 'no unity among man and wife' found in the texts above discussed. It so happens that in the case of the birth of a two-headed girl we have both the 'official' and the 'unofficial' interpretation, namely, 'No union between man and wife and diminution of the land'— forming a really remarkable parallel to the Etruscan omen.

Further testimony to the parallelism between Etruscan and Babylonian-Assyrian methods of divination in the case of birth-omens is born by an interesting passage in the Annals of Tacitus (XV, 47) that two-headed children or two-headed young of animals were interpreted by the Haruspices as pointing to an approaching change of dynasty and to the appearance of a weak ruler. Again, therefore, prognostications that present a complete parallel to what we find in the Babylonian-Assyrian texts¹⁷⁶.

---

[173] De Divinatione I 53. Cicero does not specifically state that the interpretation is due to Etruscan haruspices, but Thulin, *Etruskische Disziplin* III 116, properly concludes that Cicero who is discussing Etruscan augury in the paragraph has Etruscan augurs in mind.

[174] Among the Romans these two classes were known as ostenta publica and ostenta privata (Thulin, *Etruskische Disziplin* III 86 and 116, I).

[175] The phrase bartu or bartu ina mâti 'revolt' or 'revolt in the country' occurs hundreds of times in the divination texts.

[176] Cicero also furnishes us (de Divinatione I 36) with a most striking parallel between a Babylonian-Assyrian animal omen and an Etruscan interpretation of the same omen. He tells us that the nurse of the young Roscius observed how a serpent came and wound itself around the sleeping child. On inquiry, the Haruspices declared that the occurrence was an omen indicating that the child would become famous and distinguished above his fellows. In the same way we find in the Babylonian-Assyrian

Macrobius[177] preserves an Etruscan interpretation of a birth-omen relating to the color of newly born lambs. A purple or golden color of the lamb points to good luck. This 'purple' color corresponds to the term sâmu frequently occurring in Babylonian-Assyrian omen texts and which is generally rendered 'dark red'[178]. In the collections of the bârû-priests, many references are found to the colors of the young animals and among these we have as a complete parallel to the statement in Macrobius the following[179]:

gives birth to a young of dark-red color,—good fortune[180].

Lastly, the terms used to describe all kinds of malformations—monstra and prodigia[181], i. e., phenomena that 'point' to something show a parallel conception to the Babylonian-Assyrian viewpoint that abnormality in the case of the young of animals and of infants are primarily signs sent to indicate unusual events that would shortly happen.

That the Greeks also attached an importance to malformations, may be concluded from Aristotle's protest[182] against the supposition that a woman can give birth to an infant with the features of some animal[183], or that an animal can give birth to a young with human features. Such resemblances, he asserts, are merely superficial and he endeavors to account for them as for all

---

texts that 'if a serpent is found lying on a little child, the child whether male or female, will acquire renown and riches'. See Jastrow, *Religion* II 782 and 942, 3.

[177] Saturnalia III 7, 2 also quoted by Servius, though in a slightly modified form. See Thulin, *Etruskische Disziplin* III 76 and 102.
[178] The chief colors in Babylonia-Assyrian omen texts are white, black, yellow and dark red. See e. g., Cun. Texts XXVIII Pl. 32 (K. 3838 etc.), 4-9.
[179] Cun. Texts XXVIII Pl. 19 (K. 13443), 5.
[180] ḫud libbi, literally 'joy of heart'.
[181] Cicero, De Divinatione I 41, who correctly explains the application of monstrum to a malformation. For the etymology of prodigium, see Walde, *Lateinisch-Etymologisches Wörterbuch* s. v.
[182] De Generatione Animalium IV, 54. See above p. 44.
[183] He gives as illustrations a child born with the head of a ram or of an ox; a calf born with a child's head, or a lamb with the head of an ox. See further ib IV, 65 seq.

malformations in a scientific manner, as due to an insufficient control of the fructifying matter which prevents a normal development of the embryo. While Aristotle does not directly refer to the belief that malformations and monstrosities were looked upon by Greeks as omens, the emphatic manner in which he states that abnormalities cannot be against nature but only against the ordinary course of nature[184] indicates that he is polemicizing against a view which looked upon such anomalies as contrary to nature, and presumably regarded them, therefore, from the same point of view as did the Babylonians and Etruscans. We have a direct proof for this view however, in Valerius Maximus, who includes in his list of prodigia birth-omens recorded among the Greeks, such as a mare giving birth to a hare at the time that Xerxes was planning his invasion of Greece which was regarded as an omen of the coming event[185], or again an infant with malformation of the mouth[186]. Herodotus[187] records as another sign at the time of Xerxes' contemplated invasion of Greece a mule giving birth to a chicken with double genital organs, male and female, which is clearly again a birth omen. A further proof is furnished in a passage in Aelian[188], which reports that an ewe in the herd of Nikippos gave birth to a lion and that this was regarded as an omen prognosticating that Nikippos, who at the time was a simple citizen, would become the ruler of the island. It will be recalled that this birth-omen—the ewe giving birth to a lion—is not only of special frequency, in the omen series of Babylonia and Assyria[189], but is part of the

---

[184] De Generatione IV, 63. See above p. 44. He argues against the possibility of such hybrid creatures (IV, 55), on the ground of the varying length of pregnancy in the case of women, ewes, bitches, and cows.

[185] I, 6, de Prodigiis quae evenere Externis § I. See also Herodotus, VII 57 who represents the source of Valerius Maximus.

[186] Book I, 8 de Miraculis quae contigere Externis § 12.

[187] VII, 57.

[188] Varia Historia I 29. Aelian says that the story was told by 'the children in Cos'—evidently a rationalistic supplement to the tale, dating from a time when it was no longer considered possible to take such stories seriously. The story had become, as we would say, 'an old wives' tale'.

[189] See Jastrow, *Religion* II 875 sq.

conventional divinatory phraseology of these texts, while the interpretation based on the association of the lion with power forms a complete and verbal parallel to the system devised by the bârû-priests. The fact that the birth-omen is reported as occurring at Cos is rather interesting, because it was there that Berosus, who brought Babylonian Astrology to the Greeks, settled and opened his school for instruction in the divinatory methods of the bârû-priests. We are, therefore, justified in looking upon this circumstance as a link connecting birth-omens among Greek settlements with influences, emanating directly from the civilization of the Euphrates Valley. As another proof of the spread of Babylonian-Assyrian divination in other parts of the ancient world, we may point to the story reported by Herodotus[190] of a concubine of King Meles of Sardis who gave birth to a lion, and of the tale found in Cicero as well as in Herodotus[191], of the speaking infant of king Croesus of Lydia which was interpreted as an omen of the coming destruction of the kingdom and of the royal house. Here, again, we find (a) the familiar phraseology resting upon the supposed resemblance between man and animals and (b) the agreement in the interpretation of the anomaly of an infant capable of speaking—a birth-omen of particularly ominous significance. Bearing in mind the discovery of clay models of livers with inscriptions revealing the terminology of Babylonian-Assyrian Hepatoscopy in the

---

[190] Herodotus I § 84.

[191] Herodotus I § 85; Cicero, De Divinatione I 53. The latter preserves the tradition in its correct form Croesi filium cum infans esset locutum. The omen consists in the fact that the infant speaks as in the cases reported by Julius Obsequens (see above 52). In Herodotus the story is perverted through the rationalistic touch that the son of Croesus was dumb for many years (cf. also §§ 34 and 39) but suddenly acquired the power of speech. The story loses its point by this modification. The correct form of the story is also given by Lycosthenes, *Prodigiorum ac Ostentorum Chronicon* 65. The 'speaking' infant of which Wuelker, *Prodigienwesen bei den Römern* 20 gives six instances, was always regarded as an ill omen, prognosticating some national misfortune.

Hittite centre Boghaz-Kewi[192] and which definitely establishes the spread of this division of Babylonian-Assyrian Divination to Asia Minor, it is quite in keeping with what we would have a right to expect, to come across traces of Babylonian-Assyrian birth-omens in this same general region. That the Etruscans are to be traced back to Asia Minor is a thesis that is now so generally accepted as to justify us in regarding it as definitely established[193]. Hepatoscopy and Birth-omens thus followed the same course in passing from the distant East to the West. We may sum up our thesis in the general statement that Babylonian divination made its way from Babylonia to Assyria, subsequently spread to Asia Minor and through the mediation of Hittites and Etruscans came to the Greeks and Romans[194]. The same is the case with Astrology so far as the Romans were concerned, for whom the Etruscans again represent the mediators, while the Greeks appear to have obtained their knowledge of Babylonian-Assyrian Astrology through the direct contact between Greece and Euphratean culture, leading to a mutual exchange of views and customs.

---

[192] See the writer's article 'The Liver as the Seat of the Soul' in 'Studies in the History of Religions in honor of C. H. Toy' 164 and Jastrow, *Religion* II 742. Several of the models are now in the Berlin Museum, and will, it is hoped, soon be published.

[193] See Herbig's article on the 'Etruscan Religion' in Hastings' Dictionary of Religion and Ethics. The possibility, indeed, that the Etruscans belong to one of the Hittite groups is to be seriously considered, though naturally the problem cannot be approached until further advances in the decipherment of the Hittite inscriptions shall have been made, following along the line of R. C. Thompson's recent attempt "A New Development of the Hittite Hieroglyphics" (Oxford 1913), which unquestionably marks considerable progress.

[194] See further Jastrow, *Religion* II 320, 3.

VIII

There is still another aspect of the subject of Babylonian-Assyrian Birth-omens to which attention should be directed, and which will further illustrate the cultural significance of the views that gave rise to this extensive subdivision of Babylonian-Assyrian divination. We have in the course of our investigations noted the tendency in the collections of the bârû-priests to allow a free scope to the reins of fancy, which led to the amplification of entries of actual occurrences by adding entries of abnormalities that do not occur. In order to be prepared for all contingencies, the priests, as we saw, extended the scope of birth-omens in all directions, through entries for an ascending scale of multiple births which went far beyond the remotest possibility, through equally extravagant entries of the number of excess organs or of excess parts of the body, and through the most fanciful combinations of the features, aspects and parts of various animals in the case of new-born infants and the young of animals. The omission of the preposition 'like' in the case of these entries obscured the starting-point for such comparisons, and it was natural for the idea of an ewe actually giving birth to a lion, or for a woman to some animal or the other—a lion, dog, fox, etc.—to take root[195]. Strange as this may seem to us, yet if we bear in mind the ignorance of people in the ancient world as to the origin and course of pregnancy and the general lack of knowledge of the laws of nature, the dividing line between the possible and the impossible would be correspondingly faint. At all events, the transition from the abnormal to the belief in monstrosities that were quite out of the question and that represent the outcome of pure fancy would be more readily made. Indeed, through a

---

[195] Aristotle, de Generatione IV, 54 refers to a physiognomist who traced back all such 'malformations' (as Aristotle calls them) to two or three animals, and whose views he says met with much favor, the assumption being that such hybrid beings were produced by the union between a woman and an animal, or by crossing of animals. As a matter of fact intercourse between a human being and an animal never produces results, and the crossing of animals only in restricted cases, which do not enter into consideration in the birth-omens.

combination of all the features involved in the entries of the bârû-priests, we obtain a reasonable basis for the belief, widespread throughout the ancient Orient as well as in the Greek and Roman world and existing up to the threshhold of modern science, in all kinds of monstrous beings which find their reflex in the fabulous creatures of mythology, legend and folklore. In other words, the Babylonian-Assyrian birth-omens form the first chapter in the history of monsters. The very term monstrum, as already suggested, reflects the Babylonian-Assyrian point of view, as a being which is sent as a sign—'pointing' (monstrare) to some coming event. A monstrum is in fact a demonstration of the will or intent of a deity, which becomes definite through the interpretation put upon it. Perhaps this point will become a little clearer, if we consider some of the possibilities included in the Babylonian-Assyrian birth-omens. An ewe giving birth to a lamb with two or even more heads, or to a creature with some of the organs and parts of the body doubled and with some single is certainly a monstrosity; and it is only a small step from such monstrosities which fall within the category of the abnormally possible to supposed combinations of the parts or features of various animals in one being. We actually read in one of these texts[196] of an isbu or a young lamb having the head of a lion and the tail of a fox, or the head of a dog and the mouth of a lion, or the head of a mountain goat and the mouth of a lion; or in another text[197] of colts with heads or manes of lions, or with the claws of lions or feet of dogs or with the heads of dogs. It is only necessary to carry this fanciful combination a little further to reach the conception that led to picturing the Egyptian sphinxes or the Babylonian šedu or lamassu[198]—the protecting spirits or demons guarding the entrances to palaces and temples, as having the head of a man, the body of a lion or bull; and in the case of the Assyrian sphinxes also the wings of an eagle. Similarly, in the

---

[196] Cun. Texts XXVII Pl. 29.
[197] Cun. Texts XXVII Pl. 48.
[198] The name given to these demons. See Jastrow, *Bildermappe zur Religion Babyloniens und Assyriens* Nr. 62.

case of infants we find actual monstrosities recorded as a child with a double face, four hands and four feet, or with the ear of a lion and the mouth of a bird. Here again the step is a small one to the assumption of hybrid beings as hippocentaurs—half man and half horse—or tritons and mermaids—half human, half fish—or satyrs and fawns or monsters like Cerberus with several heads.

It has commonly been held that the conception of such fabulous hybrid beings rested on a popular belief in a kind of primitive theory of evolution, according to which in an early stage creatures were produced in a mixed form and that gradually order was brought out of this chaotic stage of creation. Berosus[199] in his account of creation according to Babylonian traditions voices this theory, and gives a description of the 'mixed' creatures that marked this earliest period of time, "men with double wings, some with four wings and two faces, some with one body but two heads and having both male and female organs, others with goat's legs and horns, with horses feet, the hind parts of the body like a horse, in front like a man, (i. e., hippocentaurs). There were also bulls with human heads, dogs with four bodies and fish tails, horses with the head of dogs, men and other creatures with heads and bodies of horses but tails of fishes, and various other creatures with the forms of all kinds of animals ... all kinds of marvellous hybrid beings". The description, which is confirmed in part by the Marduk Epic or the 'Babylon' version of creation where we encounter 'scorpion men', 'fish-men', 'goat-fish', dragons and other monstrous beings[200] as the brood of Tiamat the symbol of primaeval chaos, reads like an extract from the birth-omens in the Babylonian-Assyrian handbooks of divination. As a matter of fact, many of the hybrid beings described by

---

[199] In the Chronicle of Eusebius (ed. Schoene I 14, 18). See also Zimmern, *Keilinschriften und das Alte Testament* II 488 seq.
[200] See Ungnad's translation in Gressmann's *Altorientalische Texte und Bilder* I 8.

Berosus can be parallelled in those parts of the collections that have been published[201].

My thesis, therefore, is that the birth-omens gave rise to the belief in all kinds of monstrous and fabulous beings. The resemblances between men and animals, as well as between an animal of one species with that of another, led to the supposition that all manner of hybrid beings could be produced in nature. The fanciful combinations in the collections of the bârû-priests, in part reflecting popular fancies, in part 'academical' exercises of the fancies of the priests, formed the basis and starting-point for the theory that at the beginning of time, pictured as a condition of chaos and confusion, such hybrid beings represented the norm, while with the substitution of law and order for chaos and confusion, their occurrence was exceptional and portended some approaching deviation from the normal state of affairs. It is not unusual in the history of religious and of popular beliefs to find fancy and fanciful resemblances leading to the belief in the reality. Once the thought suggested by the manifold abnormalities occurring in the young of domestic animals and among infants firmly rooted, there was no limit to the course of unbridled fancy in this direction. Adding to this the practical importance attached to birth-omens, what would be more natural than that with the development and spread of systems of divination devised to

---

[201] E. g., horses with the heads of dogs (Cun. Texts XXVI Pl. 48, 9); an isbu (young of animal) with human head (Cun. Texts XXVII Pl. 29, 26 and 31, 8); infants with two faces, four hands and four feet (Cun. Texts XXVII Pl. 8, 10, 21-22 (K. 7093)); human face and body of a šedu, i. e., a body of a lion or bull with wings (Cun. Texts XXVII Pl. 10, 23 == Pl. 8, 6 == Pl. 15,17); infant with male and female organs (Cun. Texts XXVIII Pl. 5, 11); with the face of an ass (Cun. Texts XXVII Pl. 15, 12); isbu— probably lamb—with feet of a lion (Cun. Texts XXVII Pl. 45, 34); horse with two tails and mane of lion (Cun. Texts XXVII Pl. 49, 3 (K. 4031)); horse with human head (Cun. Texts XXVIII Pl. 31, 7); animals with two to seven heads (Cun. Texts XXVIII Pl. 33 (K. 6288 rev.)); isbu (here probably a lamb) with the feet of a lion, head of dog in front, six feet and bristles of a swine (Cun. Texts XXVIII Pl. 38, 13); with the feet of a lion, head of a dog and tail of a swine (ib. I. 15); with two heads, two tails and feet like those of a dog (ib. I. 17); two heads, two feet, hair of a dog (ib. I. 19), etc.

interpret the strange phenomena observed at birth, the belief in all kinds of monsters and monstrosities should likewise have been developed and should have spread with the extending influence of Babylonian-Assyrian divination.

Babylonian literature furnishes many examples of the persistency of such beliefs. It is sufficient to refer (a) to the gigantic scorpion-men who keep guard at the gate of the sun in the mountain Mašu and who are described in the Gilgamesh epic[202] as 'terrible', whose very aspect is death, (b) to Engidu, the companion of Gilgamesh, who is pictured as a man with the body of a bull, and the horns of a bison[203], (c) to the monster Tiamat in the creation tale pictured in art with the mouth and foreclaws of a lion, wings and hind-feet of an eagle[204], or as a monstrous dragon with the head of a serpent, fore feet of a panther, hind talons of an eagle, or again described as a serpent of seven heads[205], and (d) to the 'mixed' creatures—man, bull or lion and eagle combined—above referred to and that appear in such various forms in Babylonian and Assyrian art[206], and reappear as sphinxes in Hittite[207] and Egyptian art. The Hippocentaur in various forms also appears in the Babylonian art of the Cassite period[208].

---

[202] Tablet IX.

[203] See Jastrow, *Bildermappe zur Geschichte Babyloniens und Assyriens* Nos. 149, 150, 184 usw.

[204] See Zimmern, *Keilinschriften und das A. T.* II 503 sq.

[205] Jastrow ib. No. 120; other fanciful forms, Nos. 193-199.

[206] See Jastrow, *Bildermappe* (Gießen 1912), Nos. 36-47 (on Boundary Stones), 52-53 (dragons), 55-60 (winged human figures and winged human figure with eagle face), 61 (bull with human head), 62 (winged bull with human face), 63-64 (winged horses, winged bulls, winged sphinxes, winged human figures).

[207] See Luschan, *Ausgrabungen in Sendschirli* IV 330 sq. and 338 sq. and Pl. LV-LVI.

[208] Jastrow, *Bildermappe* No. 32 winged hippocentaur with two heads (man and lion) with scorpion tail and horse's tail and scorpions attached to the forelegs; No. 33, upright hippocentaur, head, arms and upper part of the body that of a man, lower part of the body that of a horse with two feet. Similar figures appear on seal cylinders, e. g. Ward, Seal Cylinders of Western Asia, 382, and Clay, Dated Cassite Archives, 15 and Pl. XV, No. 6. See Baur, Centaurs in Ancient Art pp. 1-4. A vast amount of material

If we are correct in tracing the spread of Babylonian-Assyrian birth-omens to the peoples of Asia Minor and thence to the Greeks and Romans, and in associating the belief in all kinds of monstrous and fabulous beings with these birth-omens and as a direct outcome of the fanciful combinations embodied in the collections of the bârû-priests, the spread of this belief would accompany the extension of the sphere of influence of Babylonian-Assyrian divination and of Euphratean culture in general. The thesis here proposed would, therefore, carry with it the assumption that the fabulous creatures of Greek and Roman mythology, as well as the wide spread belief in monstrosities of all kinds found in Greek and Roman writers, and which belief through the influence of Greek and Roman ideas was carried down to the middle ages and up to our own days, reverts in the last instance to the Babylonian-Assyrian birth-omens.

---

bearing on the representation of all kinds of monstrous beings in Babylonian, Assyrian and Hittite art will be found in Ward's valuable work just quoted, particularly in chapters LI to LV and LXVII to LXIX, but also chapters VII-XI; XV (Bird-man!) XVIII, XXXVI and XXXVIII.

IX

The thesis that the fabulous figures of Greek mythology were suggested by malformations was set forth some twelve years ago by Prof. Friedrich Schatz in a monograph on '*Die griechischen Götter und die menschlichen Mißgeburten*' (Wiesbaden 1901), in which he endeavored to show that the conceptions of such beings as the Cyclops, Harpies, Centaurs and Sirens were merely the fanciful elaborations of the impression made by actually occurring abnormal phenomena in the case of infants. The cyclops (9 seq. with illustrations) was suggested by the child born with one eye[209], the siren (11 seq. with illustration) by the abnormal but actually occurring phenomenon of a child born with the feet united. A double headed god like Janus (12 seq.) was suggested by the monstrosity of a child with two heads and even such a tale as that of the head of the Gorgon, Schaatz believes is based (24 seq. with illustrations) or, at all events, suggested by the fact that a woman gave birth to an undeveloped embryo which suggests a human head[210]. The three heads of Cerberus, Diana of the many breasts and even harpies are similarly explained as suggested by malformations or by excess parts or organs. Having reached my conclusions long before I learned of Dr. Schaatz's monograph, I was naturally glad to find that the idea had occurred to some one who had approached the subject from an entirely different point of view and without reference to birth-omens. I would not go so far as Dr. Schaatz in the attempt to trace back all the fabulous creatures of mythology, to certain specific malformations. Indeed some of his combinations are almost as fanciful as the creatures themselves, e. g., his endeavor to explain the Prometheus myth as suggested by 'extopy of the liver' (36), whereas the tale clearly rests upon the old theory of

---

[209] See e. g. Hirst and Piersol, *Human Monstrosities* 116 Pl. XXII.
[210] This birth-omen 'if a woman gives birth to a head' actually occurs in the Babylonian-Assyrian collections, e. g., Cun. Texts XXVIII Pl. 34, 24 (K. 8274).

the liver as the seat of the life[211], but the main thought that the idea of monstrous beings was suggested by actual malformations plus the factor of unbridled fancy is, I venture to think, correct. We must, of course, add to human malformations the many abnormal phenomena occurring in the young of animals in which the determining factor is again the significance attached to all kinds of malformation among human beings and animals as birth-omens. This factor must be taken as our point of departure; it furnishes a reason not merely for the rise of the belief in all kinds of fabulous creatures but also for the elaboration and the persistency of the belief and for its embodiment in the religious thought of peoples. It is because the malformation is an omen that it leads to further beliefs and fancies. The direct association of the belief in fabulous creatures with birth-omens in Babylonia and Assyria lends a presumption in favor of the same association among the Greeks. If, therefore, we can trace the attachment to birth-omens among Greeks and Romans to the Euphrates Valley, we will have found a reasonable explanation for the part played by monsters and fabulous beings in the mythology and the religion of the Greeks and Romans. Further than this, it is not necessary to go. It is not essential to the establishment of the thesis to trace all the fabulous beings of classical mythology to actual malformations. The factor of fancy would lead to the extension of the sphere far beyond the original boundaries; nor is it necessary to find parallels to all the creatures of Greek and Roman mythology in Babylonian and Assyrian literature or art in order to justify the dependence of the former upon Babylonian-Assyrian birth-omens. No doubt the Greeks, more particularly, developed the conception in their own way, adding other features to it, just as they modified Babylonian-Assyrian astrology in adapting it to their environment and their way of thinking, and just as the Etruscans and Romans modified the Babylonian-

---

[211] See Jastrow, *Religion* II 943, 1. The vulture eats the liver because it is the seat of life. The renewal of the liver is the renewal of life. Prometheus thus suffers perpetual death and is yet condemned to eternal renewal of life. This view of the liver is incidentally a proof of the high antiquity of the myth.

Assyrian hepatoscopy[212]. All that is claimed here is that the conception of monstrous and fabulous beings is a direct outcome of the importance attached to Birth-omens; and since the Babylonians and Assyrians are the only people who developed an elaborate system of divination in which the interpretation of birth-omens constituted an important division, and which spread with the extension of Euphratean culture to Asia Minor and thence to Greece and Rome, I claim that the ultimate source of the belief itself is to be sought in the Euphrates Valley.

Can we trace the conception likewise to the distant East? Dr. Bab in an interesting essay on *'Geschlechtsleben, Geburt und Mißgeburten'* in the *Zeitschr. für Ethnologie*[213] adopts the thesis of Dr. Schaatz and applies it to account for the frequent representation of gods in India with excess organs or an excess number of parts of the body—gods and goddesses with many heads, with three or four eyes, various breasts and more the like. The same would of course apply to representations of Chinese gods and demons. Bab's paper is elaborately illustrated and the juxtaposition of actual malformations with the representation of gods and demons in India and China leaves no doubt of at least a partial dependence of these artistic fancies upon actual occurrences in nature[214]. Again, however, a warning is in order not to carry the thesis too far; nor is it possible to furnish definite proofs for the spread of Babylonian-Assyrian systems of divination to the distant East, though we now have some evidence pointing to a spread in this direction of Babylonian-Assyrian astrology[215] and perhaps also of Babylonian-Assyrian hepatoscopy[216]. In a general way, we are also justified in seeking

---

[212] See Jastrow, *Religion* II 320 seq.
[213] Vol. 38 (190), 209-311.
[214] Schwalbe, *Mißgeburten und Mißbildungen bei Menschen und Tieren* I 39 also favors this view.
[215] Jastrow, *Religion* II 740 seq.
[216] See Jastrow, *Religion* II 937, 2. In Se-ma Tsien's *Memoires Historiques* tr. by Chavannes I 13, there is a reference to a monster which had the body of a man and the head of an ox, and which was born to a woman through a dragon.

for an early connection—commercial, artistic and social—between the Euphrates Valley and distant India and China, but for the present we must rest content with the assertion of the possibility that Babylonian-Assyrian birth-omens, and with this system of divination also the conception of and belief in hybrid monsters and fabulous creatures spread eastwards as well as westwards.

How stands the case with Egypt, where we find sphinxes that represent a combination of man and animal and where we encounter numerous gods composed of human bodies with the heads of animals? The question of foreign influences in the earlier art of Egypt is one that has as yet scarcely been touched, and we are equally at sea as to the possibility of very early connections between the Euphratean culture and that which arose in the valley of the Nile. The fact that the oldest pyramid—that of King Zoser at Sakkarah—is formed of a succession of terraces[217] like the zikkurats or stage-towers of Babylonia and moreover is of brick was regarded by Ihering[218] as an evidence of an influence exerted by Babylonia upon Egypt. An isolated phenomenon is too slender a thread on which to hang a weighty theory, and the step pyramid of Zoser can be explained as a transition from a form of the mastaba to the genuine pyramid, without recourse to foreign models. All attempts to find a connection between the Egyptian hieroglyphics and the oldest hieroglyphics forms from which the Babylonian cuneiform script developed have likewise ended in negative results and the same is to be said of endeavors to find any direct connection between Babylonian and Egyptian beliefs and rites and myths and despite certain rather striking points of resemblance[219]. And yet it is difficult to suppress the impression one receives that much in Egyptian art and in the Egyptian

---

[217] See Spiegelberg, *Geschichte der ägyptischen Kunst* 17; Maspero *Art in Egypt* 40.
[218] *The Evolution of the Aryan* 101.
[219] Pointed out by Hommel, *Grundriß der Geographie und Geschichte des alten Orients* I 113-129 who, however, includes much in his discussion that is doubtful, and draws conclusions that are entirely too far reaching.

religion suggests early outside influences. With Babylonia and Egypt in more or less close touch as far back at least as 1700 B. C., and with Asiatic entanglements reverting to a still earlier period, the possibility of some connection between the Egyptian forms of the sphinx—the crouching lion with the human head, the falcon-headed and ram-headed sphinxes—and the combinations of the human face with bulls and lions in Babylonian art to which the Assyrians added the wings, cannot be summarily set aside. The question as to the age of the sphinx at Gizeh—the oldest of all—is still in abeyance. Maspero ascribes it to the early Memphite art[220], Spiegelberg to the middle kingdom[221], while others bring it down to the 18th dynasty. If we accept Spiegelberg's date we will be close to the period when by general consent the Mediterranean culture—including therefore Syria, Palestine and Western Asia in general—exercised a decided influence on Egypt. It is during the time of the new kingdom that the sphinxes become frequent, as it is at this period that the tendency to represent the gods as a combination of the human and animal form becomes prominent and reaches its highest form of expression.

Now, to be sure, we have not as yet come across any traces of Babylonian-Assyrian divination in any of its forms in Egypt, but that may be due to the rationalistic character of the Egyptian religion in the 'official' form revealed by the monuments and the literature which, while full of rites and ceremonials connected so largely with the cult of the dead, is yet relatively free of magic or divination. It is possible, however, that in the unofficial popular customs divination may have played a greater part than we suspect. Be this as it may, the conception of monstrous beings may have found its way into Egypt even without the transfer of the practice of interpreting birth-omens. The thesis of outside influences to account for the Egyptian sphinxes and for the

---

[220] See Maspero, *Art in Egypt* 80.
[221] *Geschichte der ägyptischen Kunst* 35—perhaps to Amenemhat III of the 12th dynasty.

combination of the human and animal form as a means of representing gods and goddesses, is on the whole more plausible than to assume that Babylonians and Egyptians should have independently hit upon the idea of carving sphinxes to protect the entrances to temples and palaces. Naturally, we must again be on our guard not to carry the theory too far. The form given to the images of the gods by the Egyptians suggests the almost perfect blending of the human and animal, and as such is a distinct expression of the genius of Egyptian art. All that is claimed here is that the thought of reproducing hybrid and fabulous beings in art did not arise in Egypt without some outside influences. Resemblances between the human form and the features of animals may have suggested themselves to all peoples without any influence exerted by one on the other, but in order to take the further step, leading to the belief in the actual existence of beings in which the human and the animal are combined, the resemblances must have been fraught with some practical significance. This condition, I hold, is fulfilled if the resemblances—as well as all kinds of other abnormalities—are looked upon as signs sent for a specific purpose i. e. to point to some unusual happening that may be confidently expected. The monster in short presupposes what the word implies, that it is a 'sign'—an omen of some kind.

A warning may also not be out of place against connecting the belief in monsters and fabulous creatures with the mental processes that give rise to totemistic beliefs. In so far as totemism implies the descent of a clan or group from some animal, it rests in part upon the supposed resemblance between man and animals. Without this feature the thought of a descent of human beings from some animal would hardly have occurred to people, but this is only one factor involved. Ignorance as to processes of nature in bringing about a new life is an equally important factor; and there are others. But totemism does not involve the combination of the human and the animal form in one being. That combination belongs to an entirely different process of thought, though it also has as its starting-point the recognition of a resemblance between man and animals. The conception of hybrid beings is allied to that of human creatures or of animals who through defects or through an excess number of organs or of parts of the body represent striking deviations from the normal. Both classes fall within the category of monsters, i. e., they are signs sent for a specific purpose. Descent from an animal totem, however, where the belief exists, is not looked upon as abnormal, but on the contrary as the rule.

Still a third direction taken by the impression made upon man through the recognition of a resemblance between him and certain species of the animal world is represented by the belief—so widespread—of the possibility of the change of the human form into the animal. References to such phenomena are not infrequent in Latin Literatures. Pliny[222] refers to several instances of women being transformed into men. Livy[223] also speaks of this phenomenon as a matter of common belief; and it is merely another phase of this same belief that we encounter in the famous Metamorphoses of Ovid where the gods take on the form of animals, Io being changed to a cow and back again to human form, Jupiter to a bull, Cadmus to a dragon, Medea to a fish, and so on through quite a long list. Circe by virtue of her powers can change men to swine, just as she transforms her rivals into trees. Apuleius' famous tale of the Golden Ass where the hero is changed into a talking ass rests upon the same deep-rooted belief, which appears again in a modified form in the Jatakas or Birth-stories of India where Buddha takes on the form of all kinds of animals and which lead to the beast fables of Bidpai where animals are introduced at every turn who talk and act as men[224]. Even such a tale as that of Balaam's talking ass would not have

---

[222] Hist. Nat. VII 3.
[223] See also Phlegon, Mirabilia (ed. Keller) IV-X including (VI) the case of a woman turning into a man in the days of Emperor Claudius at Antiochia.
[224] See Joseph Jacobs, Introduction to his edition of the *Fables of Bidpai* (London 1888) XXXIX-LI.

arisen without the antecedent belief in the possibility of a transformation of man to animals and the reverse. In fact the talking animal in all fairy tales rests in the last instance on a metamorphosis. But this metamorphosis has nothing to do with hybrid creatures or monsters. The universal spread of totemistic beliefs preclude a priori a single centre as a starting-point for such beliefs; and the same in all probabilities holds good for the belief that men may be changed into animals and the reverse. In both, however, the factor of the resemblance between man and animals is undoubtedly involved. All that is claimed by my thesis is that the development of this recognition of a resemblance between man and animal in the direction which led to the belief in fabulous creatures and monsters, that is to say combinations of man and animal in one being, side by side with abnormalities through defective organs or parts of the body, or through an excess in the number of the organs or parts of the body is associated, wherever it is found, with birth-omens; that is, with the observation of striking or peculiar phenomena observed at the time of birth in the case of infants or the young of animals and regarded as omens. Monstra, prodigia, ostenta and portenta to use the terms employed by Latin writers. All these terms convey the idea that such phenomena are signs sent by the gods as a means of indicating what the gods have in mind, or, to put it more generally, what the future has in store. This chain of ideas and conceptions and beliefs is restricted to culture circles which have been subject to common influences.

X

The history of monsters forms an interesting division in the annals of mankind, and I should like in conclusion to call attention to the persistency of this belief down to the threshhold almost of our own days. Among the Romans up to the latest period the old law of either burning the monsters or of throwing them into the sea was generally carried out[225]. This was done on the supposition that the monster was an ill omen foreboding evil and which was sent as a punishment. Plutarch tells a story[226] which despite the skeptical attitude assumed by the narrator, shows that the same point of view prevailed among the Greeks. From the Greeks and Romans the belief in all kinds of monsters and the view that they were signs of divine anger was handed down to Christian Europe. Precisely as among the Babylonians and Assyrians, no distinction was drawn between monstrosities that actually occurred—such as infants, or the young of animals with two heads, or with only one eye, or with no nose, or an otherwise defective face, or with an excess number of hands or feet in the case of children, or an excess number of feet in the case of animals and the like[227]—and such as are purely imaginary, or in which the imagination plays at least a leading factor.

---

[225] See the references in Ernest Martin, *Histoire des Monstres depuis l'antiquité jusqu'à nos jours* (Paris 1880) 7 seq. Martin's book is a mine of valuable information on this subject.

[226] Banquet of the Seven Sages § 3. The story is placed in the days of Periander and Thales, and relates the remarkable birth of a centaur in the herd of Periander. Thales is asked to examine the strange creature, and after doing so asks the diviner Diocles, whether he does not intend to make some expiation in order to avert the anger of the gods. The diviner answers 'Why not?', and assures Thales that the birth of the monster is an omen of discord and sedition. Thales smiled and looking at the young shepherd of Periander in charge of the herd advised Periander to keep a look-out on his young men, or to provide wives for them. The intimation reflects little credit on Thales' knowledge of the processes of nature.

[227] See for actually occurring human monstrosities, Hirst and Peirsol, *Human Monstrosities*; Kitt, *Pathologische Anatomie der Haustiere* (4th ed.) I Chap. III and Guinard's *Précis de Teratologie* (Paris 1893), e. g. in the last named work, a lamb without ears (168), an infant with a caudal appendix (82), club-foot (131—still called

A learned Jesuit, Conrad Lycosthenes, published an elaborate work in 1557 under the title Prodigiorum ac Ostentorum Chronicon (Basel) in which he put together all miracles, miraculous happenings and strange phenomena from the creation of the world down to his days. This is only one of a number of compilations of this character, the significant feature of which is the jumbling together into one class, of miracles, of unusual phenomena in the heavens and on earth, of the birth of malformations—human or animal—including monstrosities and fanciful hybrid creatures,—all being viewed as signs sent by a divine power. Lycosthenes includes in his compilation the accounts of ancient writers and later travellers of peoples of remarkable formation such as the Scipodes and Monomeri (10) of whom Pliny[228] reports that they have only one foot, of people who have the heads of dogs (11), of others living in Western Ethiopia (8) who have four eyes, of the Ipopodes in Asia (8) who have the feet of horses, and of the Scythians (ib.) who have only one eye, or of people have no heads, of others with eyes, nose and mouth on the breast (9), or who have six arms, (14) or who are provided with hoofs and horns, or of women (13) who lay their young in the form of eggs.

Lycosthenes' work is elaborately illustrated and so he portrays for us these strange beings, as well as men with the heads of dogs (11), hippocentaurs (12), men with six arms (14), baldheaded women with beards, and people in the region of the North Sea who have ears that cover the whole body (13), mermaids, tritons, satyrs, fauns (10, 28, 218, 311, 317) and harpies (31). The whole army of fabulous beings of mythology and folk-lore is brought before us[229], including the remarkable creature whom

---

pied d'equin), six toes (128), a pig with five divisions of the hoof, a lamb with four divisions, a dog with six etc. (129).

[228] Hist. Nat. VII § 3.

[229] Also such omens as the speaking infant (113. 118), while still in the womb (175), the talking ox (65. 113. 118. 125. 129. 140. 146. 153. 159. 166. etc.), by the side of the two-headed swine (129), three-footed mule or horse (150. 157. 166), a five-footed horse or mule (131. 136. 171. 176), two-headed calf (180. 181. 308), lamb with

Gessner in his great work on Animals[230] describes as 'a virgin with human face, arms and hands, body of a dog, wings of a bird, claws of a lion and the tail of a dragon'. Naive credulity alone would be insufficient to account for such fancies, but if we start from the deep impression made by malformations of all kinds from the point of view of birth-omen divination, the exaggeration of such malformations through the play of the imagination would follow from the inherent fondness of human nature for the marvellous. A large part of Lycosthenes' work is taken up with the malformations and monstrosities mentioned in classical writers—Pliny, Livy, Cicero, Valerius Maximus, Julius Obsequens, Aelian, etc. which he has collected with great patience. Passing beyond classical days, he is at equal pains to put together all records of unusual phenomena, adding generally the attendant circumstances or the events that followed, which the sign was regarded as portending. All kinds of monstrosities are described, together with the date and the place of their appearance. A lamb with a swine's head (136), born in Macedonia presaged the war with Phillip which soon thereafter broke out. A double-headed ox born in the year 573 B. C. (309) presaged the defeat of the Persians. A child without arms (316) and the tail of a fish instead of legs, born in Thrace in 601 A. D., was ordered to be killed. In 854 A. D. a boy attached to a dog was born (352, see the illustration). This happened in the days of Lotharius Caesar, duke of Saxony, who soon thereafter died. In 858 A. D. (353) a monstrosity of mixed shape was born and all

---

swine's head (135. 136), swine with human head (124. 136. 138), with human hands and feet (165), two-headed lamb (138. 139. 197. 198), boy with elephant's head (125), infant without eyes or nose (141), without arms or feet (142), two-headed boy (155. 177. 315. 317), with four hands and four legs (163. 165. 172. 317), with three legs (168 and 169), with three legs and three hands (199), with four legs (175), androgynous infants (125. 135. 170. 175. 181. 187. 196. 198), twins united at the back etc., (198. 284), a child with beard and four eyes (272), a woman giving birth to an elephant (201), to a serpent (209-210), a woman giving birth to seven children in days of Algemundus, first king of Lombards (284), a boy without eyes, no arms and a fish tail instead of feet (316) etc.

[230] Conrad Gessner, *Allgemeines Thierbuch* (Deutsch von Conrad Foerer, Frankfurt 1669) 19.

kinds of misfortunes followed. Twins united at the loins born in England in 1112 are brought into connection with a victory of King Boleslaus of Poland and the death of Waldrich, duke of Saxony. He carries his chronicle beyond 1543[231] in which year a human monstrosity was born at Cracow, with flames starting out of the eyes, mouth and nose, with horns on its head, with the tail of a dog, with faces of apes on its breast and legs, with the eyes of a cat and with claws. It lived for four hours, cried 'Vigilate, Dominus Deus vester adventat' and expired. The point of view throughout is the time-honored one that the monstrosity is a monstrum—a sign sent by an angered deity, just as on the other hand as a trace of the pristine ignorance of the processes of nature, the belief continued to prevail that such monstrosities were due to the intercourse of women with demons—either wilfully accomplished by the woman, or without her knowledge. Martin in his *Histoire des Monstres* devotes an entire chapter to illustrations of this belief, which is advocated as late as the year 1836 by Goerres[232], the Professor of Philosophy at the Munich University, and even as late as the year 1864 by Delaporte in a book on the devil[233]. Such a belief which involves the possibility of pregnancy without the ordinary sexual intercourse and which has left its traces far and wide[234] in the religious history of mankind must have acted as a powerful agent in maintaining also the belief in all kinds of monstrosities that could never have occurred. The demons naturally could do anything, and thus a very simple theory was evolved to account for such monstrosities and which supplemented the older one that accounted for the simpler hybrid beings as due to the intercourse of a human being with an animal. The cooperation of the demons, moreover, was a natural correlative to the belief that deviations from the normal course of things were omens. Even Christian theology found no

---

[231] The chronicle is brought down in fact to the year 1557.
[232] *Christliche Mystik* III 440 seq.
[233] Le Diable (Paris 1864).
[234] In the doctrine of the immaculate conception of the Virgin Mary, this factor is involved.

difficulty in assuming that God permitted a demon to exercise his power over those who had through sin forfeited the Divine protection, with the result that in many cases the unfortunate mother was brought before a tribunal and not infrequently suffered death for the sin of intercourse with some demon. Martin's work, above referred to, also furnishes abundant evidence of the persistency both of the belief in monsters and of their being regarded as omens even in the scientific world down to a very late date. He tells the story[235] of the birth of twins, united at the breast, in the year 1569. The royal physician Jacques Roy was commissioned to make an autopsy and to report on the result. He closes his report with a poem, glorifying the Catholic Church and vigorously denouncing the Protestant movement. More than this, he concludes from the fact that one of the twins received the baptismal rite before dying, while the other died without baptism that the Catholic church would survive the Hugenot heresy. In 1605 twins united at the umbilicum were born in Paris, and despite the fact that the Faculty of Medicine of Paris presented a scientific report, accounting for the monstrosity through the fact that 'the semen was too plentiful for one body and two small for two', a chronicler in embodying the report of the physicians in his account presents his view that the monstrosity was a symbol of the wickedness of Papism and of Mohammedanism. Between 1539 and 1605 we have the Edict of Nantes which in rendering civil liberty to the Hugenots brought about a reversion of feeling in their favor. The tables are therefore turned, and the monstrosity is now a sign sent against the Catholic Church. The chronicler breaks out in rhyme as follows[236]:

"Je tiens que ces deux fronts, cette face jumelle,
Sont deux religions, dont l'une est qui s'appelle

---

[235] P. 98. Chapter XII, of Martin's work, ('Les Monstres Celebres'), furnishes many supplements to Lycosthenes work, including some interesting examples of Hermaphrodites.
[236] Martin p. 100.

Papisme, et son autheur est l'antechrist romain,
De l'autre est Mahumet avec son Alcorain".

The persistency of the belief in monsters even in scientific or quasi-scientific circles and of regarding monsters as omens no doubt had much to do with the fact that a really scientific theory to account for such malformations as actually do occur was not put forth until the year 1826 when Etienne Geoffroy St. Hilaire in reporting to the French Academy of Medicine on a mummy found at Hermopolis[237] and which appeared to have been that of a human monstrosity, enunciated the view which led to the science of Teratology, as a branch of modern medicine[238].

But despite the results of scientific investigation which so strikingly justify Aristotle's protest against regarding abnormal phenomena in the young of animals and of infants as contra naturam, the strong desire for the marvellous still helps to maintain at least the belief in monsters, even if the corollary that the monster is a birth-omen has disappeared.

The believers of the Middle Ages have been succeeded by the deceivers of the 19th and 20th centuries—the naive Lycosthenes by the shrewder Barnums[239] who in order to supply the demand created by the love of the marvellous have manufactured their monsters. To be sure even this is not quite new under the sun, for Pliny[240] tells us that he saw a hippocentaur which was brought to Rome from Thessalonica at the order of the Emperor Claudius

---

[237] The mummy was found in the cemetery reserved for the sacred animals, from which Martin concludes that the Egyptians shared the general belief in monsters as due to the combination of the human with the animal. It would be interesting in view of the present stage of Egyptological research to determine the exact character of the mummy which was thus destined to play so important a part in the history of modern medicine. See Martin, ib Introduction p. V.

[238] See Guinard, *Précis de Teratologie* (Paris 1854) in which a full account of the theory of St. Hilaire and of those who followed in his footsteps is given.

[239] P. T. Barnum, the famous American showman, in his Memoirs tells in a most frank manner of the manufacture of his monsters—living and dead.

[240] Hist. Nat. VII 3.

and which, as it subsequently turned out, was the embalmed body of a horse to which a human foetus had been skillfully attached. The latest companion piece to this neat bit of trickery is to be found in a description of a fish with the head of a man that was exhibited in the Crimea in 1911—fished up in the Pacific Ocean[241]!

---

[241] Amsterdamer Weekblad voor Nederland, May 28, 1911. The illustration attached to the description reveals the bogus character of the 'monster'.

XI

To sum up the results of our investigations in a series of propositions:

1. The Babylonian-Assyrian birth-omens which can be traced back to at least 2000 B. C. rest on the impression made by the mystery of a new life emerging from another.

2. A leading factor in the interpretation of the omens was the recognized resemblance—often striking—between the features of an infant and that of some animal, or of an animal to some other.

3. As Babylonian-Assyrian hepatoscopy led to the study of the anatomy of the liver, and Babylonian-Assyrian astrology to the study of the phenomena in the heavens, so the resemblance between man and animals became the basis for the study of Human Physiognomy, which when it came to the Greeks and Romans was made a means of determining the character of the individual, just as Babylonian-Assyrian astrology when transferred to Greece and Rome was applied to the individual as a means of casting his horoscope, i. e., for determining the general course of his life.

4. This same factor of the resemblance between men and animals in conjunction with the ignorance as to the processes of nature led to the belief in all kinds of hybrid creatures, composed of human and animal organs or features.

5. This belief underlies the fabulous creatures of Greek and Roman mythology, and also helps to explain the representation of gods as partly animalic in Egypt, in India and in China.

6. The recognition of a resemblance between man and animals is universal, and besides leading in connection with birth-omens to the belief in the actual existence of beings composed of partly

human and partly animal organs or parts of the body, developed quite independently of such associations also in three other directions, leading on the one hand to the belief in the descent of a clan or group from some animal, and on the other to the belief in a transformation of a human being into an animal and vice versa, and thirdly to the Beast Fables of India in which beasts that talk like human beings are introduced.

7. The theory set forth in Berosus of a time when mixed creatures of all kinds existed reflects the fanciful combinations found in the collections of the bârû-priests.

8. The Roman view of a monster as a 'sign' (monstrum), sent as an indication of some event of a disastrous character, is directly traceable to the Babylonian-Assyrian point of view of malformations of all kinds and deviations from the normal as birth-omens.

9. From Rome this view passed over to mediaeval Europe, where under Christian influence the monster became a 'sign' sent by an angered deity as a warning and as a punishment for sins.

10. The pristine ignorance of the course of nature, leading to the assumption that conception could take place without sexual intercourse, had its natural outcome in the belief that women giving birth to monstrosities had intercourse—wilful or unknown to them—with demons as emissaries of the devil, or with the devil himself. This attitude served to maintain the belief in monsters down to the threshhold of modern science.

11. The Roman law of burning the monstrous birth or of throwing it into the sea was maintained for a long time and led also to the punishment of the woman who through supposed intercourse with a demon had given birth to a monster.

12. The view taken of monsters as a sign sent by an angered Deity had much to do with preventing the rise of a scientific theory to account for actual malformations of all kinds.

13. The rise of Teratology as a branch of medical science in the 19th century represents the closing chapter in the history of monsters, which is thus to be traced back to Babylonian-Assyrian birth-omens—one of the three chief branches of Babylonian-Assyrian divination that all made their way with the spread of the influence of Euphratean culture throughout Asia Minor and westwards to Greece and Rome, and that may also have passed to the distant East. Porta, who in his Della Fisonomia dell' Huomo (Venice edition, 1648, chapters XIII and XIV, or Latin edition De Humana Physiognomia, Frankfurt 1618, chapter IX) ascribes to Plato the opinion that a man who resembles an animal is likely to have the traits of that animal, appears to base this view on such a passage as Phaedo § 31, referred to in the note, and which is given as the reference in the German translation of Porta's work. The passage, however, hardly admits of this interpretation, though it would appear from Porta, who evidently does not stand alone in his opinion, that from Plato's view that according to the life led by a man his soul will be transferred into an animal having the traits manifested by the individual, the corollary was drawn that a man who resembles an animal has a soul which shows the traits of the animal which he resembles.

www.ingramcontent.com/pod-product-compliance
Lightning Source LLC
Chambersburg PA
CBHW071743090426
42738CB00011B/2549